Beyond Sex:

Tantra

Tanja Diamond

Cover concept and design by Max Bellasys and Tanja Diamond

Cover created by Max Bellasys

Author photo by

Katie McCullough Simmons

katiemsimmons.com

Published by Modern Tantra™ Press

9 Lake Bellevue Way,

Bellevue, WA, 98005

www.ModernTantra.info

ISBN

978-0-578-05013-3

Printed in the United States

About the author

Tanja Diamond, "The Tantra Teacher", C.Ht, NLP, creator of Modern Tantra™ and Tantra for Business™ is a Life Strategist with a specialty in Business, Spirituality and Sexual Intimacy, She has been working in the US and abroad, expanding human consciousness for the past 25 years.

Having lived and studied all over the world, Tanja has been fortunate to have many spiritual teachers in both conventional theories and the esoteric philosophies. Many formal credentials in applied science and psychology, certifications in energetic disciplines and several uncanny intuitive gifts make Tanja a dynamic force.

As the creator of Modern Tantra ™, she and her team empower and educate people all over the globe to live lives more completely while being full engaged.

Modern Tantra ™ is the path to Life Mastery. It is taught through 5 levels and it includes the Tantra of Awareness, Tantra of Self, Tantra of Relations, Tantra of Business and the Tantra of Life Mastery. Modern Tantra™ believes that your foundation as a human needs to be solid in order to move through life in a meaningful and delighted manner.

Tanja is the most practical and easily understood Tantra teacher today, flexible in any format, using humor to make the sometime awkward subject of sex and spirituality educational, enlightening and fun.

Tanja is legendary for putting sizzle and intimacy back into sexless marriages. Working with couples that have not been sexual for 10 or more years, she has created sexual dynamos in one afternoon.

Tanja's takes on the boardroom with Tantra of Business™ and her Inner Circle Program, teaching the most powerful business tools the corporate world has ever seen. Tantra of Business explodes companies to the top of their game at warp speed.

An endlessly curious nature has taken Tanja into the depths of the human mind and spirit, expanding past boundaries that have halted others. Her rock star style of teaching has touched, thrilled, inspired and empowered the lives of thousands.

Email: Tanja@LearningTantra.com

Website: www.LearningTantra.com

Tanja is available for speaking engagements, personal coaching and workshops.

Table of Contents

Acknowledgements

Acknowledgement: To admit the reality, existence or truth of.

You would think after writing a book that the acknowledgements would be an easy task, but I find this the daunting part of this whole project.

What happens if I miss someone critical? What are acknowledgements really about?

I have read over several dozen books and their acknowledgement pages today, having to admit that I have never ever looked at one before I had to write this. They come in all shapes and sizes, very curious indeed.

Is the acknowledgement page about gratitude, is it about ego, is it about making other people happy?

Going with the definition above, I would have to say that I am who I am today because of every one of you. The truth is we are all connected, our thoughts are able to interconnect, and we have the same passion and aspirations to be all that we can be.

This book is a tribute to us all. It is a creation to inspire every one of us to action. We have a planet that is in trouble, we have people on it who desperately need to feel authentically and to experience life fully.

Thank you for the time you give to read this book and the time to support my team's mission.

To my best friend Craig, what do I say… thank you isn't enough. You have always been here for me and believed in me all the way.

To Ethne, my daughter, who has sacrificed her time with me, I can't give you the time back, however, it is my fondest desire to be an inspiration to your planet to assist its healing so you can experience its complete brilliance and find expansive love and authenticity. You are my inspiration and one of my greatest teachers.

To Max, my warrior, my heart, my one, my everything, I find breath with you. I find the truth with you. I find arousal so exquisite its fires purify my soul. You inspire and challenge me to find the razor's edge and then dance upon it with abandon.

Tanja, Sept 2009

Author's notes

There are times throughout the book you may run into a word which may not appear in the dictionary. One such word is intentful. I have consciously used these words and ask you to consider them fully and openly.

This book contains thoughts and ideas which may cause you to react strongly. That is great. Embrace your feelings as they come up and experience the moment. When you find yourself triggered by my words or thoughts consider them deeply. Is this something you get triggered by often; is this an issue from your past?

Life will always hand us ways to work through our challenges, the question is are we up for it?

I empower you to write to me if you are particularly happy, sad, or angry about anything you read. Please feel free to communicate with me via email. Go to to Tanja@learningtantra.com to email me.

I look forward to your feedback.

Be amazing,
Tanja

Foreword

What is Tantra?

My definition of the concept of Tantra is, quite simply:

"Tantra is the ultimate love affair with yourself and all of your existence. In the process of igniting your internal flame, you come to experience all ordinary moments as extraordinary experiences. Immersed in that experience, you realize that you embody the divine, there is nothing else to need or want but that moment."

Tantra, however, is anything but simple. It is a spiritual practice as well as a scientific one.

Tantra explains that it is possible to reach a spiritual path while engaging the world around us. No need to sit in a cave somewhere. Tantra is for the householders of society. Tantra is for people who have to work, and choose to have families and active lives. I daresay the old masters didn't know quite how active we were going to be today moving at Mach-1 with our cell phones in our ears.

I created Modern Tantra™ to bring a relevant educational system, or technology if you will, to those of us who need and desire to be awakened from our apathetic slumber, and to embrace a conscious way of living.

Tantrikas, those who have studied Tantra, maintain that suffering isn't caused by lacking some understanding of the divine. Suffering is caused by lacking knowledge of how the world functions. Until one can understand the subtle forces of the working world, one cannot hope to regulate them and thereby regulate our internal environment.

Tantra consists of highly organized study in various disciplines, or Tantric formulas if you will, and the purification of mind and heart. It is the weaving of the ethereal and the physical together.

Most people today are not going to learn the classical art form of Tantra. We are neither committed enough nor will we make the time. We can however use some of the philosophies and exercises to create more Tantric moments. Creating Tantric moments will make the difference between simply existing in a dreary experience or living and loving your life to its fullest capacity.

By learning Tantric philosophies we are able to take delight in our senses. We are being present and focused in what we are able to "feel" physically as a way to celebrate our existence. It is the mastery of living in the now, fully embracing each moment with all that you are, using the spontaneity of non-thinking, simply experiencing.

Tantra has been around for 6000 or more years. The literature is so vast, with the majority written in Sanskrit, it would be impossible to study even a small part in one's lifetime. It is a widely misunderstood and misinterpreted art form. Although it is all encompassing, it has a particular systematic approach.

The complete rituals in Tantric text are never fully disclosed; therefore in the pursuit of learning Tantra one must find an adept or master. Rituals and studies are passed from master to student as they have been for centuries.

As a science, as well as an artistic discipline, Tantra increases the speed of evolution in the practitioner throughout their lifetime, ever expanding their knowledge and experiences.

The practitioner is always a student and revels in the magic that presents itself daily. The goal is to activate the Shakti, the power of the divine force within, or power of the soul. Without access to Shakti, true spiritual illumination is not possible.

Tantra was, long ago, divided into 3 schools for a more systematic approach to learning. The school of Kaula (divided into a right and left-handed path) is the one that uses material objects, the senses and the body.

This path enabled everyday household members to experience the divine by using everyday life, and all that lives within as a form of spiritual development. Amongst the 64 art forms were dancing, cooking, flower arranging and the art form of union. Sexual union is the art that most of us are interested in today.

This can in fact be so unbalanced that Tantra in many places has become synonymous with sex work, erotic massage, orgies, polyamory and a host of other things that just aren't it. "Tantra teachers" are popping up by the dozen and telling people they need to take their clothes off or engage in sexual activity and this stands to counter the base ideas of Tantra.

Neo Tantra as it's called deals mainly with the using Tantric, Kama Sutra and Taoist techniques to enhance sexual feeling and the experience of sexual intimacy.

Though Tantra does address the subject of sexuality for spiritual growth, less that 3 percent of the literature is relegated to that subject.

It's believed in classic Tantra that if two people cultivate and practice the art of Tantric union (intentful sexual intercourse) that their combined energies would form a pathway to the divine. Their joy and bliss would fill their household with love, and that, in turn, would make their children happy and flow over into the whole community. Everyone would benefit from this practice of conscious loving.

Tantric union enables healing to take place as well by using the powerful energy of creation to blast through ego, fear, and illusions. Tantric union is not a path to sexual indulgence or self-gratification, and like with anything in life, due diligence must be followed if looking for a teacher to train with.

Tantric union isn't just a matter of techniques. If that's all it took, everyone would be Tantric masters at loving. There are enough books on sexual technique to keep you reading for a lifetime. It takes a spiritual relationship with oneself first, in order to create that path with another. A spiritual relationship makes sexual union a magical space, not the other way around.

Learning to be conscious of our sexual energy can enhance not only our lovemaking, but also our entire lives. Sexual energy is the most powerful force that we have; when harnessed it can be used for more creativity and life enjoyment.

We teach 5 levels to Life Mastery in the Modern Tantra™ Program. Tantra of Awareness, Tantra of Self, Tantra of Relations, Tantra of Business and Tantra of Life Mastery.

Modern Tantra™, is a practice we can embrace today, in the lives we are living. Embraced and lived in our lives filled with technology, complications, conveniences, at our crazy pace, and in our new family structures.

I know my life is an amazing journey that continues to evolve beyond what I could ever have imagined as I continue my spiritual journey with Tantra. There are few limits when you have the tools to unleash the power of the universe within and out.

Though this book is about the basic foundations and philosophies, it is the very place one must begin the journey to a new experience.

I welcome you to fully revel in this book and use the philosophies, tips and practices to create your own heaven, nirvana or whatever you wish right here and now, in this moment and beyond.

Enjoy and be amazing,
Tanja

Chapter One

Arousal of life… Come on, get turned on!

Arouse: to awaken from sleep, to excite. Arousal, the act of being aroused.

Arousal is a way to experience living, from the tastes we taste, to the smells we smell. We can choose to be acutely aware of these or completely tune them out. When we tune our senses out, life can become dull and bland. We then may seek to find experiences outside of our self to enhance and reactivate us.

Looking outside for arousal leaves most of us feeling lacking. This empty feeling leads to more searching and more emptiness and we desperately wait for something to pull us out of our bleak existence.

As we become dulled to our senses we lose the ability to feel sensation, to hear sounds, see colors, taste things and to experience pleasure in our bodies as we once did. I believe we become depressed in this state. Sexual depression in the form of low libido for women and erectile dysfunction for men is seen as medical- I see it as spiritual. I see it as a lack of living in full arousal.

Even further I feel we not only suffer from sexual depression but emotional and intellectual depression as well.

As humans we have the potential to be aroused in many different ways and through lots of different channels. One of the greatest gifts we have is the ability to experience life from a profoundly deep place, and living in arousal is the key to accessing those depths.

As children we came into the world in arousal of everything and insatiably curious. We lived for the moment of new sensations, reveling in how things felt, the texture in our hands, ears, mouth and anywhere else we could explore it. Intellectually everything was new and we expanded our minds almost minute by minute.

We looked at green and saw hundreds of shades as our eyes feasted on the sights around us. Our taste buds exploded in response to the food placed in our mouths, we were acutely aware of all the sound around us. Life was a delight to be engaged in.

When we hear the word arousal as adults we tend to limit this expression to our genitals. The genitals are usually the last place arousal is lost because of the evolutionary need to procreate. The arousal in this area of our bodies can be a joy or a frustration. We see it as joy when we have some way to celebrate it, as an annoyance when we are single or experience frustration when the sexual energy is stuck there.

When I am out on stage teaching to live in full arousal the question I get is how do you concentrate if you are running around horny all the time?

I am not horny all the time. I am in full-blown arousal all over and throughout my entire body. This is not a feeling I would ever want to get out of, or lose. I want to make it even bigger and bigger. I love living my life on fire, milking every ounce of each experience fully and completely.

Learning to move your sexual energy up out of the genitals and through your entire body takes all the frustration out of the crotch and leaves it freed up for creativity and to live life fully engaged. One of the practices of Tantra is the ability to do this.

Sexual energy is potent and when used through our body it enlivens us in a way we didn't know was possible. We want and we need to live in arousal. Living in full body, unabashed arousal of all our senses can help us live a life that we truly experience deeply and in connection to everything around us.

Come on, jump on board, your arousal is free, fun and bound to raise some eyebrows!

How to:

Gather friends and/or a lover and some really yummy food. Get foods that delight the senses with color, smell and texture that you can eat with your fingers even if it's messy (that's more fun anyway). First feast your eyes on the food, really drink it in, and use your eyes to notice everything. Then feel the food with your fingers, roll it, squeeze it, caress it, watch others have fun as well. Then feel it with your lips, top and bottom, inhale as you do this for maximum experience, touch it to your tongue. Before you put it in your mouth really desire it, breath your arousal up into your mouth, play, and laugh. Once you put it in your mouth really savor it. Use your whole mouth and tongue, feel the juices slide down your throat, breathe.

Repeat and let others feed you and you feed them. Make an event out of the whole thing.

Chapter Two

Beliefs are holding you back...
Reprogramming your brain

Belief: trust or confidence; conviction or opinion; something believed or accepted as true

The beliefs that we have define how we live. We may think that our circumstances create our life but that's a small part of the picture. Our circumstances are caused by our beliefs about our self and life and those beliefs then impact our decisions. The outcomes of our decisions create our circumstances.

Beliefs come from our programming that our parents and society have instilled upon us. We are born to absorb information and we do so from the time we are in the womb. Once born we absorb our parent's words and facial expressions, their gestures and their feelings.

We never question our beliefs as a rule, we just go about living our lives believing what we believe, and being stunned that our lives are turning out like they do. In a sense we are victims of our belief systems.

If your family has told you that the family legacy is to get fat, you will indeed get fat. With that legacy usually comes being admonished for eating certain things. A typical conversation might look something like this: "You know potato chips are fattening; if you keep eating them you'll just get fatter!" Contrast that with the thin people who absolutely believe that they can eat anything they want and still stay thin. And so they do.

There comes a certain amount of personal responsibility when you begin to understand that you can actually break free of your old patterns and old programming no longer a victim adrift, you can set your own path.

So why is it important to experience your own experience instead of just living your beliefs?

While we live in the beliefs that were handed to us, we frequently find ourselves in conflict. The typical cause of this suffering is that our own personal authenticity butts up against the programming we were handed. For instance, your family expectation is that you become a doctor. And so you diligently go to school to become a doctor. In the meantime your soul is that of a poet, and so you struggle trying to do what your family believes you should do while leaving behind your personal truth.

This type of inner conflict will lead to depression and an experience of dissatisfaction in your life. Most people at this point choose to medicate themselves in some format or other to alleviate the pain of internal conflict. Using drugs, alcohol or others forms of medication isn't going to end the conflict - it will just add other issues. Finding your personal truth is a freeing experience, unfortunately for many it is a long time in coming.

Living a life free of internal conflict is living the life that you were designed to live, a life experiencing more joy, more expansion, less illness and dis-ease.

So how do you find your internal truth and leave your programmed beliefs behind?

The journey is simple, as with most things in life, but it requires transferring your attention from what you're thinking in your head to what you're feeling in your body.

I know of a man who retired from scientific research and was looking for a new career. One day I happened to read an ad on Craigslist about a pony party business for sale. In jest I shared it with him. The subject was dropped until two weeks later when the man wondered aloud if the business was still for sale. I looked up the ad and placed the phone call because I noticed that the man was grinning from ear to ear just contemplating this seeming madness.

How could I tell that this venture was the right one for him?

I knew because he was so clearly feeling the experience of the business in his body. His body, his grin, his posture was in joy, and that showed his personal truth. Mind you, he knew absolutely nothing about ponies or business, yet he's having the time of his life living the experience of his truth and doing well.

How to:

Grab a pen and paper and write down what you believe about your life in the areas of work, money, love and sex. What's going on now with these topics and what do you really desire? DO you believe you can have everything you desire or is that just for other LUCKY people? Pay attention to tension in your body or emotions that come up as you ponder these questions. Go ahead and really feel what's going on - you will receive some very interesting answers.

Chapter Three

Conscious Breath... Wake up!

Consciousness: A sense of one's personal or collective identity; Special awareness of or sensitivity to a particular issue or situation.

I am asked every day, what is the single most important ingredient in becoming a fabulous lover or enlightened being? I tell everyone the key is Breath-Conscious Breath.

Conscious Breath is the very thing you need for optimum physical and mental health, life vitality, longevity, spiritual illumination, sexual vitality, growth and stamina, sexual mastery and spiritual and sexual enlightenment. We even teach Conscious Breath as a foundation in our Tantra of Business courses.

Without *Conscious Breath* you will be ruled by *unconscious* programs placed in your body and mind by parents and other authority figures while you were growing up. These unconscious programs lead to action on your part that do not always serve you the way you think they do.

For example, most of us feel we want to parent a little bit better than our parents did. It's human nature to try things our ways. Yet once we are parents ourselves, we can hear our parent's words coming out of our mouths. We are at times even shocked because we swore we would never say that.

I know that Conscious Breath doesn't sound sexy, but the results are by far the sexiest thing you will ever experience in this lifetime. Something as simple as breathing the correct way will improve your health, your sexual organs, your orgasms, your stamina, your spiritual sexual connection, your past traumas and your love for yourself and others.

With advanced breath work you will be able to achieve pleasure you had no idea existed in the world. I believe that most of you are experiencing only about 2 percent of your capability of pleasure right now. I certainly know this from my own experiences.

It is not possible to advance in Tantric studies if you do not engage in Conscious Breath practice. No matter what other techniques you learn they will be dull and lifeless without the ability to manipulate energy with your breath. Energy follows breath. The ability to use your breath with specific intent allows you to influence energy all around you. It is with these breathing techniques that you can learn to increase the flow of energy through your body and flow that energy to others as well.

If you were being monitored medically, you would see physiological changes happen the instance you took your first Conscious Breath. Emotionally you will start to notice differences very quickly and profoundly as well. As you become aware of the power of Conscious Breath and you begin to use the different breathing techniques for specific purposes it is like having your very own personal healer on board.

Every day I hear that by learning Conscious Breath my student's lives are changed forever. That not only are they engaged in everything they do more fully, but their health has improved, their feelings about life, and of course many are on the path to experiencing bliss in sexual loving. Conscious Breath really works and the ease and simplicity is profound. The only thing stopping the amazing results from happening to you would be you not doing the practice at all.

Whether you are on a spiritual quest, just wanting to feel better in your life or on a journey to immense sexual pleasure, Conscious Breathing is the beginning of your path, the middle of your path and ultimately the big driving force at the apex of your bliss.

Conscious Breath is power. It is power in your hands to make the most of your life.

How to:

Breath awareness. Start by closing your eyes and just paying attention to the breath you have now. Feel it go into your nose and down your throat. Don't change anything just pay attention to what's happening right now. Let your face relax, your jaw, your shoulders and your stomach. Follow your breath as it easily and effortlessly goes in and out of your nose. Just let go and follow. Do this anytime you need to relax or focus for a couple of minutes.

For a more detailed practice in Conscious Breath get my Conscious Breath V-book (video embedded e-book) from my website.

Chapter Four

Doing versus Being... The Mind Bender

Doing: to perform or execute; to fulfill or complete.

Being: to exist

We are a society of doers, and we are in fact completely revered for our acts of accomplishment.

Today saying "I'm stressed because I'm busy" is a badge of honor that we wear proudly. In all this doing and multi-tasking, our lives pass by in such a hurry that we barely experience anything at all. Life passes us by in a blur. As our list of accomplishments grow and our to-do list gets checked off, somehow we still feel unfulfilled. We believe that it's because we haven't accomplished enough, and that right around the next corner, right after the next project, lays our satisfaction.

This outward expression of satisfaction creates an internal hollow or void that aches to be filled. So consequently we fill it with more **doing** stuff. For those people who are seeking enlightenment the path to **doing** is just as pervasive - with just another guru, just another workshop, and one more book to read before you get it. The **doing** never stops. In the rush to achieve enlightenment, to become open hearted, to find love, we have lost our innermost knowledge of what **being** really means.

Being is a state, a self state that was accomplished before we were even born. To simply **be** in our state is one of the most simple yet seemingly complex of ideas. I know what you're thinking right now: "What do I do to **be** in my state?" If you're laughing, more power to you, because you're actually **being** in this moment. If you're one of those analytical people, right now you're saying "This book is full of crap." Go ahead - be brave and read on, maybe clarity is on the way.

There are moments in our lives that simply are. In those moments we can simply **be**. "To **be**" is the act of surrendering to the experience you're involved in. In that moment you aren't trying to get anywhere, you aren't trying to **do** anything: you are solely the experience you're having. For example: **being** in love. This is actually a self-state. It's only when we're trying to make it about someone else, as in "we fell in love" or "out of love", that it becomes a **doing** word rather than a **being** word.

How to **be** instead of **do**? **Being** is a state that engages all aspects of human potential; it could be called an "active mediation". When you **be** in the moment you feel it fully and completely, with all your senses and emotions. When you're busy **doing**, you're focused on the outcome and the accomplishment which takes you out of your experience and into your logic. The outcome is your accomplishment rather than the experience.

When I invite people to do a healing circle in my classes I ask them to stand in front of a stranger about a foot away and gaze into each other's eyes. For the most part this is a very terrifying and difficult process for the uninitiated. What frequently happens it that people start to **do** instead of **be**. Men will start to assess whether the woman is attractive and if so should they flirt with her; and women will start to guard from advances they perceive might be coming. Two men across from each other prepare for battle and posture. All of these things are acts of **doing**. To change this to a state of **being** I ask people to start breathing, relax their bodies, and just have the experience instead of seeking an outcome. Most agree that this is challenging at first, but once in the state of simply **being**, peace and easiness prevail.

In a way it is letting go of personality and coming into a state of soul.

Coming into the state of soul might sound a little "out there" for some of you but hey, you paid for this book, so **BE** here and keep reading.

How to:

The next time you are having a conversation with someone pay attention to them completely. Don't give feedback (nodding or encouraging) and don't go to your brain about what you are going to say. Feel what they are conveying, watch their body posture, listen to the sound of their voice, breathe with them. **BE** in that moment completely.

Chapter Five

Expansion and Contraction... The Universe in Motion

Expansion (to expand): to spread out; unfold. To increase or become increased in size, quantity or scope.

Contraction (to contract): to shrink and draw together.

There is nothing static in the universe. Things are always contracting and expanding, inhaling and exhaling, being created and destroyed.

I believe that a lot of our misery as humans comes from a place of wanting to stay still, find a routine and stick with it. We're looking for a perceived safe result. If our experience yesterday was satisfying and not too scary we want to recreate it today. It is fear that keeps us desiring to control our destiny. We attempt to control the outcome, and yet to do that is the most artificial experience in the world. No time is like another no moment can be the same; it is contrary to the laws of nature and the universe.

We create these moments of stasis to ensure happiness or at the very least sameness. It is as though we believe that the static is preferable to the unknown, because we really feel at a core level that everything could get worse instead of better.

What we need to realize is that there is no such thing as a static anything, and we have traded in expansion for an ever more restrictive life. As we become more fearful and contract ever more we lose the joy and the desire to live our fullest life. We become dull and sick, and lonely in our solid shell as if walled off from everything there is.

We can see the difference between people who are expanding and others who are contracting. Body posture, voice, movement, expression and vitality are dead give-aways.

People who are contracting have a "no" attitude, they slump, eyes downward, fearful of making decisions, fearful of being open to potential.

Expansive people are light, open, joyous and excited about saying "yes" to the world and all its possibilities.

Being static is unnatural as a person has to actively do something to remain in that state. They need to actively create contraction over and over again. They remember all the pain in their lives, they are suspicious of motives of others, and they will not risk their heart or feelings. They perpetuate their contraction by living a life in fear. They become victims of their own perceptions. It is a cascading effect.

When living in expansion one still has experiences that cause contraction but they don't cascade, they are simply blips in the experience.

Contraction has a physical sensation as well as an energetic component. When you feel sad or hurt you will curl inwards and not inhale fully. The act of not breathing solidifies the negative experience in your physical body by creating an anchor or memory of that pain or fear. You can then retrieve it at will and live the experience over and over again , believing you are still in the pain or fear, though it is long gone and over with. You will remain stuck, as close to static as you can be. This is serious misery. Since nothing is static, the universe or you will provide an event to create change... hey how about a life-threatening illness?

So what to do to live in expansion?

The foundation of most of what I teach has to do with Conscious Breath and body awareness.

The very act of breathing fully causes more expansion than contraction in our bodies. If we have a fright we can take a full breath and let out sound - otherwise we anchor the event into our bodies. If we lose our voice and our breath we will be terrorized.

Practice expanding your physical body and your breath in micro-practices daily. Micro-practices are done through-out the day a few minutes at a time. Learn to feel where your body is tight when you remember an event. Breathe into that tightness and let go with sound and movement, and you will start to feel energy return and expansion happen.

But be careful, living in expansion takes guts, cause everyone else thinks you're nuts to be so happy. Just ask me how I am and I will tell you I am amazing!

And we all deserve to feel amazing, self deprecation serves no one.

How to:

Take an inventory of your daily life. How routine is it? Do you feel life is passing you by quickly and nothing new ever happens? When was the last time you chose to do something out of your comfort zone? Well then make a point of doing something this week that is different. Take a new route to work, get lost on a drive this weekend. Expand out of your norm and have fun! Live life out loud!

Chapter Six

Forgiveness… I don't buy it

Forgiveness: to excuse for a fault or offense, pardon; to stop feeling anger or resentment against.

I know I am going to be roasted for this one but hear me out before you fire me.

I believe that we use this term of forgiveness before we have stopped to even give it much thought. It has become a catch phrase in the world of enlightenment. To forgive is to be somehow closer to God or bigger than someone who has not forgiven. Forgiveness is supposed to benefit us and make us feel whole again.

I think the concept of forgiveness is a tad egotistical. Let me explain with a story.

One upon a time there was a man who felt he had hurt me at the end of our relationship. He wrote me an email that said he "hoped I would be able to forgive him one day". Now as a teacher of spirituality I immediately thought, Oh of course I forgive him, that's what I am supposed to do. Then I started to contemplate what this process really meant and how it would feel and what repercussions it would have when I did it.

I was part of leading a Tantric community at the time and I would write emails to them about being Tantric and process and experiences I had on my journey. I wrote the following.

Today someone who hurt me asked me to forgive them. I was of course going to do so and then I started to ponder the following questions.

Since he has asked me to forgive him would he actually be waiting for the time when I did? Would his life be less as he waited, perhaps even years till he received my forgiveness, or was his query to me simply lip service?

Did he need me to forgive him to go on?

And then I wonder how amazing it was for him to hurt me and then ask me to be bigger than he was and make him feel better by forgiving him. Was that really the right thing to do?

As I pondered these questions I came to the realization that simply forgiving him was not enough and not the answer.

So I told him...

"No I do not forgive you. I feel that to do so would be egotistical. There would be an implication that somehow I had the power to ease your burden of accountability. If you feel like you hurt me or wronged me, you need to come to your peace with that. I can not absolve you.

As for my part, I also feel that to forgive you would be telling the Universe that I knew better than it did about the master plan. That the very thing that happened between us was wrong in the grand scheme of life. I am in no position to feel that what transpired is wrong, to laugh at the gifts bestowed upon us in this time.

So, no I do not forgive you, but I shall accept what has happened and move forward in gratitude of our experience, the pain and the pleasure. Thank you for our journey."

I feel acceptance might be a higher journey than forgiveness and I understand that this shall cause some ruffled feathers, but please ponder it if you will.

How to:

Think about something that has happened in your life that you still have feelings about. What would change if you could come to a place of accepting what had happened; even find gratitude about the experience? See if you can find a place within yourself to see the beauty of that outcome.

Chapter Seven

Gratitude... The Power of Real Change

Gratitude: thankfulness

I know that love is the word that gets all the action and credit for doing the most good in the world. I hear daily if we could all love each other more then there would be no warring; I don't agree.

The feeling of gratitude or gratefulness for one's life is extraordinarily powerful. Gratitude is a positive attitude or emotion in acknowledgement of a benefit that one will receive or has received. I have seen people I know use the power of gratitude to manifest abundance in many aspects and live extraordinary lives.

In my coaching programs the first thing I teach is to move towards gratitude in daily life. My students, clients and I have found it can have a profound effect almost immediately.

There have been studies done that show the physical, emotional, and spiritual benefits. People who feel grateful have a better sense of well being. Grateful people are less depressed, less stressed, happier and more satisfied with their lives.

It is my belief as well as others' that gratitude is even more powerful than love. I see gratitude as an empowered and conscious choice, one that requires action to happen. And once that action occurs on that magnitude the outcome can change history. It can certainly change your outlook and perspective in an instant.

Take an inventory of how you feel daily. Do you spend a lot of time being frustrated or upset that everyone seems to have it better than you? Do you tell yourself that if you only lost weight then everything would be great? Do you spend a lot of time thinking" if only" statements?

Being stuck in the loop of lack and "if onlys", is damaging your life. It is definitely keeping you stuck where you are, and all the complaining in the world or hoping things will change is not the answer. Being in gratitude of what you have and what you are today is a practice. Turning your thoughts to the positive is neither what you typically see role modeled nor what you would generally do. It is said that 90 percent of what people say and think is negative.

I would like you to contemplate for a moment the concept that what you focus on is what you get. Then you need to ask yourself, are you living the life you are focusing on? Being grateful for what you already have, and taking care of the things you already have, shows the world that you are ready for the big time. Live the life you want to have right now by being in gratitude.

There are so many things to be grateful for in our lives. We live in an amazing time where we understand that the thoughts we have are energy. We understand that when we use our thoughts with intent we can create outcomes for ourselves, and that these can be positive or negative outcomes. You are ultimately accountable for what happens to you.

I know that really makes some people upset. It's hard to understand when horrid things happen to us or to our loved ones that somehow there was someone accountable.

I had a situation once that was very challenging to see any way to choose to be in gratitude. I had suffered a closed head injury from an automobile accident, I had just gone through a divorce, my uncle died, my aunt died, my mother was dying, and I was diagnosed with an incurable illness, all of this occurring within a 3 month period of time. I was feeling very sorry for myself. In fact I was wondering if life was worth living in the chronic pain I was having.

I had just turned 30, and what I was thinking of as the worst year of my life turned out to be the turning point for me. I got a tattoo that year, my first ever. It says "no guts - no glory" to remind me of my courage. I was there when my mother apologized for her mistakes and I apologized for mine. I was there for her when she died. I discovered a will to live through really horrific physical pain, I became my own medical advocate, I grew a sense of deeper compassion for others, I learned to be vulnerable and ask for help.

I became grateful for small things going well. The sound of my cat purring when he was on my pillow, the fact I had another day to be alive, that I had a business where I could work only 20 hours a week and pay my bills, the sun on my face and my ability to sing.

I made a gratitude list and I used it every day, sometimes several times a day. I would tell everyone I ran into something wonderful I saw in them. I focused on the moments when my pain was less instead of more. I focused on being amazed by life.

I developed my personal mantra that I still use today. "Thank you Universe for my most amazing life!" and when I say it my heart fills so much, tears of gratitude flow down my face. It works every time.

My incurable illness is no longer with me and I live every day in gratitude of the worst year of my life. Gratitude has the force to heal all facets of your life. It's hard to be miserable or disappointed in anything when you live in gratitude.

How to:

Right now-just as things are in this moment- take an inventory of the things you are grateful for. Write them down and place them somewhere that you can see the list. Every day, read the list and feel the gratitude. You must feel emotion in your physical being to create the extraordinary change that this can bring. When you realize how grateful you are in your life come up with a short verse or a mantra that you can say any time you need a reminder of your amazing life.

From my journal

Today started off without my usual ability to take a moment and focus on gratitude of the great things in my life. Too little sleep, the dog whining, my daughter complaining about her clothes and having to go out in the cold with me, blah blah blah… Of course realizing that the moment we enter into expectation of how things should be we lose the ability to be in the moment of what is.

Tantra is a practice of presence.

So as I stood outside with my morning breath, needing to pee, daughter complaining about her clothes being itchy and the dog running off and not coming back …. I took a breath… I release the tension in my abdomen, felt the expansion happen and looked at the trees, heard the morning sounds of the birds and the smelled the rain.

As soon as my focus shifted I felt the wonder of this art form I study and teach.

Tantra was created for real people living in a real world. Real worlds have family and things happening. No time to sit endlessly in silence, or meditation. The meditation of Tantra takes an active form in our daily lives.

My heart opened and I felt the love I have for my child, the compassion for her plight about texture, my dog's desire to just be a dog, and my gratitude to live in a wonderful place with trees all around.

I still had morning breath, still had to pee, and all of my life's hectic pace was waiting just outside of this moment....though in this moment I had peace, gratitude, love and my awareness that I can be in this moment anytime I choose. We all can.

Chapter Eight

Healing your Sexual Self... Creating Empowerment

Healing: to restore to health, or to regain health or soundness.

When it comes to healing we have a plethora of options these days. We have traditional, naturopathic and alternative venues. We can talk, move, sound, vibrate, scream, dance, sing, twirl, rebirth, breathe, meditate, see colors, drink elixirs, spray scents, and a whole lot more.

Even so the area of your sexual empowerment lags behind in the healing world. Sexual empowerment isn't even talked about in polite company. If it were, how does one go about getting or finding it? Sexual healing is the solution.

Sexual healing... who needs it and what is it?

Sexual wounding occurs from the time of birth and continues on throughout our lives.

The first time our diaper is changed and the smell is bad, the diaper changer is going to have that yuck look on their face. As a baby who reads facial expression you will see the look on the face of the person you love the most and the area it is directed at and this will have an impact on how you feel about your sexual center. Of course the way you are respected, touched and educated about your body thereafter will influence you as well.

Wounding around sexuality doesn't always look as obvious as sexual abuse; it can be subtle as your first sexual rejection. The point is we all have wounding and it impacts all facets of our lives, not just our sex life and our relationships.

Sexual healing isn't just about sex.

It's about your empowerment, self love, life, and letting go of the fears that keep you from being the amazing being you are. You were born with the birthright of experiencing immense pleasure within your body, to play and to delight in sharing fully with others in a conscious way.

When abuse, ignorance or the carelessness of others has taken away your capacity for pleasure, your safety, and the ability to receive love, it's hard to live a healthy life.

Being unable to fully enjoy your sex life or totally give yourself over to your lover, being sexually unsatisfied or sexually dysfunctional, feeling disconnected and lonely, can leave you frustrated about a lot more.

Sexual dissatisfaction can lead to depression, illness, loss of self esteem and addictions.

In this country right now, 58 percent of women are uninterested in sex. Mind you, this isn't about desire of sex itself. Mainly it's the quality of sex as they have experienced, and many women would rather go shopping than engage in lovemaking. More and more men are losing interest in the sex they are experiencing as well. Porn is taking over the lives of way too many people.

There is the myth that women aren't as sexual as men, and that they lose their sexual energy and drive as they age. This simply isn't true. It is true that due to ignorance, abuse and other issues, women aren't getting what they need or want sexually and intimately. Or, if they are getting what they need, they have emotional and physical issues that keep them from the enjoyment that is their birthright.

Both men and women are laboring under cruel labels society has imposed upon them surrounding their sexuality. Labels like frigid and premature don't serve any of us.

Men don't need to lose their sexual potency as they age. They can be set free of anxiety regarding the timing of ejaculation or erection firmness. Men can learn to regain or retain the vigor of youth, to increase performance and extend duration of their own orgasm, as well as have multiple orgasms.

It serves no purpose to feel shame, guilt, anxiety, fear, or embarrassment around our sexuality. We cannot live our truest expression as human beings while tucking away our sexuality, our desire, our sexual passion. Do not attempt to fool yourself into thinking you are fine, and that sexual desire is simply for other people.

What are we going to do with all this information and how do we heal our sexual self?

Through the years of assisting people through some very serious issues surrounding their sexual wounding I have come to know these things.

One, talk therapy alone will not get you all the way through this process. Two, energy work alone will not get you through either and neither will a plethora of other modalities on their own. By the time people get to me for help they have spent thousands of dollars and hundreds of hours on any and all of these modalities.

You need a blend of talk, energy work, Conscious Breathing, eye gazing and bodywork to make a holistic approach to the issue of healing your sexual self. These all need to occur at the same time.

Society is in desperate need of this work, and there are very few people who are capable of providing it at this moment. I embrace the day when we can easily have our entire body receive the help and healing it needs, with honor and dignity.

How to:

Every day, either morning or nights, for at least 5 minutes hold your genitals with one hand and your heart with the other. That means to place an open palm gently and lovingly over your vagina or penis and the other hand open palm between your nipples against your chest. Breathe and relax. On an out breath send love to yourself, love to your heart and your sex organs. Imagine love if you cannot feel it right away. Do this for at least a month and feel the changes that occur. Don't be concerned if at first you feel nothing but a sense of being corny. There might come a time when you feel tears or other emotions. Just be with them.

Chapter Nine

Intent and Integrity... The Path of Impeccability

Intent: an aim or purpose; the state of one's mind at the time one carries out an action; meaning or significance

Integrity: steadfast adherence to a strict moral or ethical code; completeness, unity

These two words, intent and integrity, are pretty fundamental when it comes to living a life of consciousness. Though they are separate in their meanings one cannot be lived without the other. To live a life of intent is to live with purpose and to create meaning in the world, to live in unity. If you are able to imbue your exhalations with conscious intent you will move about your life in a very magical way indeed.

We can use intent in many ways. We can touch with intent, breathe with intent, think with intent and be with intent. The difference between how you touch your lover and your friend is only the intent used. My favorite place to explain this is when talking about love.

I find it interesting that people want to qualify their state of love. According to most people there are many types of love. There is the love you feel for your children, yourself, your parents, family, friends, pets, shoes, cars, sports teams and lovers.

I feel as though love is love. It is an emotional state brought about by our own volition. We have the experience, we manufacture the chemicals in our bodies, we have the feeling and we choose to give into its expression or not. There are no different kinds of love; there is only a difference of intent. The love I am feeling for my daughter has intention of family, there is no intent of romance or sexual charge placed upon it. The love I have for my beloved has the intent of romance and sexual encounter placed upon it. Therefore once the emotion (chemicals) of love is there, love then becomes an intentful action, an action that you can intend to sustain and cultivate or not.

Another way to use intent is in our thoughts and habits. We can have thoughts that we intend instead of just unconscious thought. It does take some practice but it is well worth it. Since thoughts have power we may as well use them in a way that benefits us. What do you spend most of your time thinking about? Do you manage your thoughts or are you just a victim of them randomly coursing through you?

Intent is the conscious action of spirituality. The intent you project will be the results you will achieve.

Now how about integrity? What does living in integrity mean and how do we achieve this?

We have very few role models that we can recognize as living lives of intent and integrity. Our children get their role modeling from TV and the internet. Scary isn't it?

When defining integrity I like the idea of completeness and unity instead of adherence to a strict moral code. I say this because I think that we should seek our own balance and anything that is completely rigid isn't going to do anything but encourage us to falter. We need to create integrity in our lives and live by our own code of conduct. Our code of conduct should reflect our highest values as conscious human beings.

Higher values are things such as truth, compassion, gratitude, and impeccability.

Living in integrity requires intent. It is the action of being in alignment with your values. Every day one must make the decision of intent to put one's values in the forefront of the day. Nothing else will suffice to live impeccably.

We will never live empowered lives if we don't respect ourselves and we will never respect ourselves until we are living our lives from intent and integrity.

Get with it, the fate of the world is waiting!

How to:

Take a look at the things in your life that make you feel yucky. Perhaps there are promises you have made and broken, debts outstanding, things you have let slide and now stress you out when you think about them, damage you have done to someone else that was never repaired. Make catching up with your integrity list a priority. Let go of the things from the past if there is no possible way you can rectify it, and then make a serious effort to rectify the other things. Put up a list somewhere you can see it and check off the items as you get them done. You will feel so good!

Chapter Ten

Jumping around Looking Wacky! Everything is Vibrating

Jumping: to move discontinuously

Wacky: eccentric, crazy, silly

This is not just about a funny chapter name, no sir... it's about self empowerment. How does jumping around and looking wacky empower you?

Our physical movement is something that has fallen by the way side in modern times. Sure a lot of us work out; we move our bodies from place to place as we walk to our cars to commute to our jobs. We might be even more conscious and ride a bike for transport. Perhaps you are a dancer and are thinking right now, "Hey I move, I dance!"

The truth is most people don't move for the pure joy of moving once they pass the age of 5. Motion of joy and spontaneity are a thing long gone, replaced by systematic and rigid movement, or little movement at all. We move our bodies in machines and forms. These forms or positions were created by someone else and choreographed for bodies that might live in a different rhythm than ours. Either way we aren't moving in accordance to our own feelings and desires. We are not in free expression, abandoned to the moment and that experience.

The importance of unformatted movement is not only in the joy it brings but in the presence of the moment it creates. As we jump around, or twirl, or do whatever we please, we release tension, expectation and energetic blocks. If we insist on remaining motionless we will create conflict in our beings. Stagnation of the body creates stagnation of the mind and spirit. This is a living death: there is a heartbeat and basic body functions but no real life or full arousal of existence.

Eventually the basic physical functions start to break down and soon there will be no motion of the internal or external body. We see this in young and old here in the US, and it's an epidemic of physical and spiritual apathy. We need to move, we need to sweat and we need to abandon to the joy of free motion every day. Let go of the fear or worry about what others think as you move to your own expression.

The most compelling reason to move might not be as obvious as you think. We hear doctors tell us to move to lose weight, move to stay younger, but the biggest reason to move is an energetic one.

Energy follows breath and movement. Everything is energy and everything around us is in motion. Energy connects us to everything in the universe and when we can use our personal energy effectively we are a conduit for whatever we might desire. As we move our breath becomes more natural and we use more capacity the more we breathe.

Physically we become engaged in the world around us as our senses come alive. As our senses come alive we start to feel our existence more deeply and profoundly, and we break out of our apathy and depression. Out of our depression we once again live in joy and curiosity of the things around us and we begin to dream. Our dreaming takes flight and we move our bodies in delight of the visions of possibilities. These visions when coupled with intent create our new realities. These new realities are about our successes and empowerment. We become the children we were naturally born to be. We become free of our physical restrictions and our spiritual restriction; we soar into our lives and fulfill our purpose.

So what are you waiting for... get up and jump around and who cares how wacky it seems, you are on the edge of your dream... and your dream in turn is waiting for you as well.

How to:

This is super easy. Get some great music and just start moving. Play it loud. Let go of what you might look like and have fun! Or skip down the street and twirl with the wind. Start stretching and yawning in public. Whatever you do, get moving with freedom and be an inspiration to others. Make sure to move all your body!

If you desire a form to move into I suggest Hsin Tao. My friend Ratziel Bander was handed down this beautiful art form. HSIN TAO is an extremely powerful self-healing and regenerative technique that was practiced secretly inside the Shaolin Monastery of China. I swear by it and so do many people around the world.

Chapter Eleven

Knowledge is Overrated... Do some Unlearning

Knowledge: the state or fact of knowing; familiarity, awareness or understanding gained through experience or study

I know, you are wondering if I have finally lost it with this chapter. How can knowledge be overrated? We spend most of our lives learning things. We are respected and in some cases revered for the amount of knowledge we have.

People have tended to give me their respect for of all the credentials I have and the letters behind my name, so how can I make this absurd statement about knowledge?

I am a perpetual student, the first one to say that I will never quit learning. Nevertheless there is a potential problem here that we do need to address.

In the process of all this education we are amassing, all the self help books we read and all the TV we watch, we are stuffing our heads with things. We are adding other people's opinions to our minds, we are in turn spouting out their opinions as our own. We do the quizzes and the tests and we occasionally even go through an entire book and do the process, for a short time.

All of that makes me wonder why there are so many wounded and unfulfilled people still around. I mean if all it took was a technique or an exercise then how come we all aren't enlightened already? Why aren't we healed and complete?

Part of the problem is that very few people follow the protocols they read about. For example in this book, there are tips and things to do to assist you in your process. Most people won't even have gotten this far when reading. Others of you will get here but not do any of the suggestions more than a few times. Then there are the skeptics and the people who believe all these things work for other people but not them.

If you are simply going to piece meal someone's protocol it is not going to work for you at all. There comes a time when you need to let go of the knowledge you think you have and actually do something new.

The fact of the matter is knowledge can keep you from actualizing. The knowledge you have can come into conflict when you are discovering something new. Knowledge has a purpose when we needed to know what berries to eat and how to stalk our food. We needed it for survival. Today over learning can lead to indecision and to conflict and inability to actually hear with new ears and see with new eyes.

Don't get me wrong. I am not suggesting we ban college and refuse to learn anything. But learning and gaining knowledge is a doing thing, and doing is in your head. Most of the stuff we truly need to know is going to come to us from **feeling** in our selves. We can't trust ourselves while in a head space because our gifted minds can rationalize anything rather expertly to suit our purpose and that is precisely the problem. Our minds have been programmed by others and we are smart enough to pull out the answer we think we want if we use this method.

Unlearning to use our heads and instead going back to a natural state of feeling will make life more powerful and the decisions we make more authentic. We are complete humans and we need to use our entire bodies and its resources to truly make unified and completely authentic choices.

"Knowledge is in the head and Mastery is in the being" so do yourself a favor here. If you like what you have read in this book, decide that you are going to put it into practice and commit to a 6 month plan. Let go of what you think you understand and know (knowledge) and take a journey with me into the unknown. Journey with me in this book to places where you will encounter your true feelings and the ability to know without a doubt you are living from a place of your personal truth and power. This will not be my opinion of your state, it will be your journey, and this book and I are simply your tour guides.

How to:

Starting with the first letter actually DO the how tos. Engage some friends or perhaps use this as your book club book where you will do the steps together. Some of the practices require a commitment of at least a month; engage some help to be accountable. But whatever you do, get started and get ready for huge change.

Chapter Twelve

Love is a self state… Be in Love Now

Love: deep affection and warm feeling for another; the
emotion of sex and romance/ strong sexual desire for another;
a beloved person; a strong fondness or enthusiasm

There is a lot of talk about this subject and everyone knows that
loving yourself and others is paramount, but it's a mystery to me why
we place such immense importance on this word and feeling.

Love is touted as the be-all and end-all of feelings. We hear about it in
fairy tales from as early as we can remember. We do our utmost to be
"good" enough to hear it from our parents. We actually live and die
emotionally for the words "I love you," and what it represents to us to
be loved or to have love withheld from us.

Love can be used as a weapon and as leverage. Most of us understand
this at a core level because we have had it happen to us or have done it
ourselves. We have used love to get what we want and need, or maybe
not even used love, just the words… I love you. The power is immense.

Love however is simply an emotion. It's a flood of feel good chemicals that can ebb and flow through us, and if we allow it to do so, it can affect our relationships.

"I love you, but I'm not in love with you…" What the hell does that really mean? We choose to love someone. We choose to let ourselves share the state of love we can be in at any moment. It isn't as though we once loved someone and that love somehow disappeared never to be found again. The chemistry of love may have changed, but we still have our intent and actions.

That said love isn't the sole reason to have a relationship with someone. I know that sounds crazy but there are so many components that should be in place to create a great relationship. Most arranged marriages work out better than our self-picked love ones. After all there is a 61 percent divorce rate in the US; love isn't working out that well apparently.

I can attest to the fact that in most of my relationships which ended, falling out of love wasn't the problem. They ended and we were still in love. Go figure.

We frequently confuse love and sexual chemistry. I think that's because when we are young we are told that sex is something people do when they are in love. Young girls are told that way too often. The messages are confusing and so when sexual desire creeps up there is no language or understanding about what's happening … and then that magic word **love** comes in to play.

Young men will feel intense about the girl and say the words they need to say to get their sexual needs met; young women will ask the men " do you love me" before they let their bodies go forward into sex. I don't believe anyone is really attempting falsehood, I just think because there is no education we are hurting each other through ignorance. We have no way to talk through these intense emotions and feelings.

Love, love love, all we need is love, or so the song goes. I think we need a lot more. Although love is not the only answer for choosing our partners, it is the answer we need for ourselves.

When we learn to become our own beloved we stop looking to fill that space of unworthiness in ourselves.

We then can fill up our own selves and lose our old sense of desperation. Coming from that experience when we do meet someone we are already in a state of love and we can come from a place of sharing instead of needing something. We can freely give the love we have to another without reservation or fear that the love will be taken away or not reciprocated.

Once we realize that we are the creators of love, that wonderfully delicious and compelling feeling, we can then experience it whenever we desire. We understand it is not attached to a thing or person, or anything besides ourselves, and so we can love with abandon through our whole lives.

We can then choose to pick our beloveds not because THEY make us feel something we are so desperate to feel, but from the sanity and completion of our own whole being.

Contemplate being in a state of love, whenever you desire, for as long as you desire. Imagine being in a state of love with your partner for the duration of your relationship, because you are the creator. You are not the victim of your partner disappointing you and causing the loss of love you hold so dearly. By your action you choose to love every day, no-matter what.

How to:

Close your eyes and envision a time when you felt huge love. It can be for anything or anyone. A sunset, a baby, a pet, a beloved, a vacation, it doesn't matter what it is, as long as you can feel the presence in your heart and it makes you warm and feel love. Amp this feeling up, really experience it, let your heart fill. When you are deep in the feeling bring both your hands to your heart and give that huge feeling back to yourself. You can do this anytime, and as you practice more, notice the bigger will be the smile on your face, anytime, anywhere.

There are some of you who will find this practice distressing as you may feel physical pain in your chest. Some of you will cry as you release grief and sadness- just stick with it, this is healing work and all is normal. As you break past the walls you built to protect yourself you will be able to go out and you will love again soon.

Chapter Thirteen

Manifesting your Desires... Create Abundance

Manifesting: Clearly apparent or understanding, obvious; manifestation: An indication of the existence or presence of something.

Manifesting is not a new thing. It has however, been brought to the attention of the main stream population over the past few years with the movies such as; "What the bleep do we know, The Secret and The Hidden Mysteries in Water." Research has found a connection between the power of the mind and what happens in our life and the results are speaking for themselves.

The process to create what we want in our lives is called "manifesting" - the bringing of ideas and desires into physical form. Manifesting becomes a self empowerment tool when it is applied to realizing our desires. This is done through the law of attraction.

All sort of celebrities like Anthony Robbins, Harv Ecker, Oprah, and Eckhart Tolle, are using manifesting daily in their professional and personal lives to achieve outrageous results. This ability to manifest our dreams is not limited to the gifted; anyone can posses this ability, all it requires is an understanding of how to put it all together.

One of the most amazing manifesting icons of our time is Darren Jacklin, A World Authority on Making Your Dreams Come True. He truly embodies the heart and soul of connecting people, and using energy and intention to create for himself and others the dreams that we are meant to live. One of the secrets to his success is his heart and his knowledge that we live in abundance and we all deserve the best life has to offer.

There are many paths to manifesting though they all start with the need to harness our mental energy and put a focus on it for a specific outcome.

One of my own personal manifesting tactics is in the process of utilizing sexual energy for raising my personal vibration, and giving me focused energy, intent, and clarity.

I say that the bigger the energy is and the more potent the intent behind it, the more powerful the message to the universe. There is no bigger energy than sexual energy which is how we create life. Utilizing sexual energy is about harnessing the intensity of arousal and keeping it inside your body instead of expelling it out through normal sexual exchange. Though this may sound like a more exotic way to manifest, I can assure you it is a lot of fun to learn and practice.

Let's start with some basics of manifesting

The law of attraction is a universal law which states that, "what is within, is without." It means that what is first created inside the mind will eventually become an outward reality.

Our negative self talk and old programming can be powerful manifesting tools as well. If these are the things you are focused on, you can well understand why you might be in the position you are today. Ask yourself right now…

What do I believe about my life and circumstances?

What do I believe about myself?

Make a list of thoughts that run through your head about your life, relationship, money, your sex life, and other facets that are not where you would truly desire them to be.

Making an assessment is a really imperative start.

Once you can honestly look at what you are creating now in your life, you can start to use these next principles to change it all around.

To start manifesting follow this process: **Ask, Believe, Release and Receive.**

Asking…In order to manifest your desires you must ask for what you want. Some people get stuck here and it is good to know that there are ways to get through the fog. Asking is not enough. You must be so crystal clear in your vision you can actually see, hear, feel, taste, touch and utilize all your senses when visualizing your desire.

Believing… It cannot be if you do not believe that it can be. The universe works in accordance with your thoughts, so if you really do not believe that you can do something then you can't. Your internal dialogue can keep you from believing you are worthy, or that you can have what you desire. You are the only thing holding you back.

Releasing…This is a process of trusting the laws of attraction and your clarity and intent. Once you have achieved clarity and precise asking and believing of what you are manifesting then you need to let go. Do not go looking for it, do not try to speed it up, do not spend time wondering where it is going to come from. The universe is more than capable of doing what you ask without your interference.

Receiving… You must be ready, willing and able to receive your manifestations: in your mind and in your spirit you must know that you deserve and that you are capable of bringing your desires from the unseen to the seen. This can be tough for some people. Practice living what you desire. Own the car, or boat, have the boyfriend or girlfriend. The process works, only doubt or lack of worth can hold you back.

Some tips from the pros.

Rule #1: Align the Desire With Making Progress In Your Spiritual Evolution.

Rule #2: Align the Desire For the Greater Good of All.

Rule #3: First Deserve, Then Desire.

To summarize, desires that are strong, spiritually oriented, and beneficial to others and which you have worked hard to realize are the ones that the Universe is most likely to help with.

Living in gratitude each day of what you have right now and thanking your divinity is an excellent way to stay positive and in the moment while on your journey of manifesting your desires.

Remember that even your breath in the world is impactful and that remaining aware and conscious of everything around you will allow you to see the opportunities that are constantly there.

There are different types of formulas to follow out there in the world of manifesting. Some people enjoy ritual and trappings, some people enjoy the process of writing vision boards, journals or painting.

But no matter what format you use to start your process, I encourage you to do it today, right now!

How to:

Follow the steps outlined in the chapter above and have a really great time with all the new things that are going to come up in your life.

I wanted a new office chair that was like my old one but with arms. I also wanted to find it on the side of the road for free. It took 2 days. I wanted to drive a yellow 2008 FJ cruiser for free, it took 6 months. The man of my fantasies who felt the same about me, 24 years (people are a little tougher and I really went for the top). I have many more stories about manifesting items big and small.

What do you really desire?

Chapter Fourteen

Nourish Yourself and Live in Pleasure

Nourish: to provide with food or other substances necessary for life and growth; to foster the development of/ promote.

Pleasure: Enjoyment or satisfaction, a source of enjoyment, one's preference, wish or choice

Is it too much to ask to live a life that is pleasurable versus having a few random pleasurable moments?

What would that experience be like?

Do you live that life?

Are the things you experience, touch, look at, smell, hear and feel enjoyable to you?

Living a life in pleasure is a wondrous event. Living like this is an experience that supports the growth and enhancement of not only the people who are living it but also the people who surround them. In fact I know this is healing for the families and the communities they live in.

Or perhaps this sounds a little too hedonistic to you. Maybe you sneer at this thought and feel that a life lived in sacrifice and toil is a more appropriate use of your life and has a higher virtue attached to it.

We have a few belief systems in place that idolize sacrifice. From the programming from our parents we are told that relationships take sacrifice and hard work - and if that isn't enough we go out to jobs that we dislike and are told we should be damn glad we even have a job to go to. Buck up!

Perhaps that is why so many people will act out in damaging ways. I remember one of my ex's telling me that he did so much in our relationship that he deserved something just for him, like a treat. Of course I had issue with this since his idea of treating himself was escorts and booze. I realize that this is an extreme case but take a look around and see what you might be doing to get that need met.

If we decide that living in pleasure is not a bad thing to do, how different would we live our lives?

The word selfish has a bad rap and the word selfless can be downright scary. Most people were raised by mothers who have no idea how to care for themselves. Our mothers have been taught by their mothers to sacrifice their own lives and pleasure for others. It is a badge of honor that has been worn far too long.

Why do we think suffering is a worthwhile pursuit? Why do we feel when we enjoy our lives we are somehow doing something wrong or not worthy?

Living a life that nourishes your soul and self is an act of inspiration.

It is an inspiration to your own senses and an inspiration to those who live around you. Someone who lives in pleasure feels abundant, they are filled up. They move through life from a place that is inspired and nourished and therefore can easily give to others.

When you only buy things that give you pleasure then everything around you is pleasing. The money you spent on it feels like you gifted yourself. From the pen that you use, to the colors you paint your room; there are endless ways to promote pleasure.

It takes some conscious thought to make sure you spend your money and time in this thoughtful way. It is a life practice like so many other things, and this one requires you put your desires on the table. It requires you to give some thought about the things that you really enjoy, things that you might not normally consider when making decisions to purchase the basics in your life.

How about that toothbrush, your soap, your clothes, your linens, dishes and of course the list can go on and on. If we can give ourselves permission to make these things a priority in our lives perhaps we will give even more importance the bigger things in our lives. If we are already living in abundance and pleasure then we would know we deserve the best in life. Would we then demand more from our relationships and our career choices?

How to:

Go about your home and make a mental inventory of the things that really give you pleasure. Now look at the other things. What's the balance like? How many times do you handle something on your desk, at home or work that makes you happy when you touch it? Now go and buy or find something that gives you pleasure, this can be something little or big. For instance I love the color orange, so I love to use orange colored pens.

Chapter Fifteen

Orgasm and Women's Sexual Satisfaction... Are we Orgasm Obsessed?

Orgasm: the highest point of sexual excitement; ecstasy

Everywhere you look sex is with us. It is used in the media and advertising and in most magazines to one extent or another. The main topic on everyone's mind regarding sex is about orgasm.

There are hundreds of books written about orgasm and the ability to guarantee her satisfaction every time and an equal number on his orgasm being bigger. We seem to equate orgasm with sexual satisfaction. I understand that most men have their sexual self esteem tied up in their ability to give a woman an orgasm, and trust me women feel the pressure of that as well. The most intimate and loving act we share has turned into a goal oriented experience and everyone is suffering.

To a woman who has never experienced an orgasm it can be seemingly the most important sexual goal. She labels herself broken and suffers when her partner tries so very hard to make it happen for her. The pressure for both of them leads to resentment and ultimately a lack of desire to engage in the act itself. Women can become depressed and their desire for any form of intimate expression can plummet.

Orgasm for women has more to do with feeling intimately connected than with the special techniques that all the books out there would have you believe. If all it took were fancy fingers then everyone would be easily orgasmic. Women surrender to the pleasure they feel when they feel connected and safe with their partners.

For men the inability to give a woman an orgasm can be a frustrating and humiliating time. The struggle to want to please her before he is pleased becomes a chore, and sexual encounters lose their sense of fun and play.

Even for couples or individuals who regularly experience orgasm it can become a form of medication or even a means to an end instead of a pleasure in itself. The act of love making can become routine and mechanical, lacking any true expression of intimacy. In this situation both parts of the couple can be wondering if this is all there is.

The reality is great lovemaking isn't about the goal of both parties getting to orgasms. In fact there should be no goal at all. Goals are better left for sports and business.

Love making should be about play and exploration. Tantra can teach you how to slow down the process of lovemaking and to use arousal for extended periods of time. If you do this it will keep your sexual energy high and in your body instead of attempting to get rid of it. This in turn will allow you to have a very different time in the bedroom and out.

Once out of the mindset that sex has to be about an end result then there are endless opportunities for play and being in the moment of whatever there is.

If the average woman takes 45 minutes to become aroused enough to orgasm, this can be daunting to most couples who already feel there isn't enough time in the week for quality love making. Using Tantric philosophies they can see each other in a different way and connect together without the goals and agenda.

Sexual satisfaction then becomes about the quality of intimacy you share and the time in between making it to the bedroom is just as important. Intimacy is the thing most couples crave and mistakenly think that sex and orgasm is going to fulfill.

Being intimate is about being present with your partner throughout the day. Listening and caring about what they are feeling and thinking. Doing things that show your love and how special you are to each other ranks high in the satisfaction department. Sexual satisfaction is about the everyday things more than it is about the orgasm.

Even though satisfaction is not about the orgasm, orgasm is an important part of our lives. It is really too bad that something that is so beautiful and healing also can be a source of concern.

Women are feeling a lot of pressure because we have been told there are so many orgasms to achieve. There are clitoral, g-spot, u-spot, a-spot, cervical, multiple, energetic, spiritual, and of course we are now told we need to ejaculate as well.

When most women are struggling to achieve a clitoral orgasm they can be downright daunted by all the rest. I am here to say, please never feel less than others because you are only having one type of orgasm. There are women I know who are not orgasmic at all and yet they still very much enjoy sex with their partners. Yes you can learn to have them all, but it is not a necessity of life or sexual satisfaction. If you are struggling remember that there is help just a phone call or email away.

How to:

Grab a pen and paper and write down the things that make you feel satisfied in your love making. Perhaps it is when your partner tells you how lovely you look naked, or maybe when they use your name while in passion. If you believe it's all about the orgasms look for other things that give you fulfillment: a touch, a look, a special word. If you are solo how do you get your sexual satisfaction? You should be your own best lover no matter what, single or partnered. Find your satisfaction outside of the orgasm and you will be a very happy person indeed.

Chapter Sixteen

Present... Experiencing in the Now

Present: existing or happening now, a moment or period in time intermediate between past and future: now

This always gets me riled... "hey, just go with the flow" "it's all good", "I just go where the moment takes me"...

I believe these statements are gross misinterpretations of what living in the now and being present in the moment represent.

There are people who think that living in the now somehow means to let go of any action on their part and they instead just meander through existence with no call to anything but the aimless meandering. If you let go of action and simply flow with an experience without intent or conscious involvement you will end up in places you may not desire. Allowing yourself to just drift along is lazy and apathetic.

Being in the moment is an active experience. It requires participation and focus. You have to show up and become present. Bring your awareness to what is occurring at the moment, not what you are hoping will happen, or day dreaming about the future.

Like having a conversation with someone- there are those people who actually listen and then there are those people who are formulating what they are going to say next and miss most of what is happening now.

In most instances going with the flow turns into becoming a victim of circumstance. This is one of the reasons we see so many "spiritual" people living in poverty or not achieving a life goal or mission. While they may float around from one experience to the next there is no course set, no achievable outcome. And while it may be true that there were monks and yoginis wandering around with no material possessions that were on the path to enlightenment they had set a conscious intention to follow this path of simplicity. It didn't just happen by circumstance.

Modern Tantra™ is the essence of presence and being in the moment in your complete authenticity. It's about making conscious choices to create a particular path in your existence. Living with intent is a meditation of action.

There are words we hear in these spiritual times, like "showing up," "being present," "living in the now," and I believe that we can get pretty confused about what they actually mean, so let's take a moment here to talk about them so that we get clear.

Showing up means to turn your total attention to the moment at hand, to bring your entire being to the situation you are in. Your mind is fully engaged, your senses active and your energy focused directly in the action now. It is the same as being present in the moment.

Living in the now is an active state of being present with what is happening directly in your life at this moment. You are an accumulation of your past experiences but the past is over and if you are looping in the past and living from past decisions and fear then you are not living in the moment.

By the same token if we are worrying about what might happen we are future-tripping and not living in the moment either.

I have a tremendous amount going on in my life. I have a child, a relationship, two businesses, a team to manage, books to write, videos to produce, clients to teach and workshops going on. I also still have all the mundane tasks at hand as well. It can get pretty hectic and there is a whole lot of goal setting and multi-tasking going on. One might think that there is no way to practice living in the now around my house.

My living in the now practice consists of micro practices all day long. I am moving from one task to another with equal focus and attention. For instance, when I answer a call from a client, I switch gears and engage my ears and become very tuned into the situation. I let go of anything else I am doing and BE there. When my lover reaches over to stroke my back I stop the other things I am doing, look deeply at him, appreciate how amazing he is, feel his hand on my back, smell his cologne and hear his voice as we eye gaze for a few moments of connection. At that moment I am not contemplating the past, or fast forwarding to the future. I am living in that moment and these micro practices will get me there.

How to:

Start right this moment to bring all of you into THIS moment of presence. Bring your breath, your mind and your body right here, right now. Feel the temperature of the room on your skin, hear the sounds around you, experience the furniture you are sitting or laying on, smell the smells, feel the weight of this book in your hand, relax into this experience. If thoughts come through allow them and then move back into THE present. Experience your body as you focus here now.

Chapter Seventeen

Questions for your Journey

Questions: an expression of inquiry that invites or calls for a reply; a subject open to controversy; a difficult matter, a problem

This chapter is dedicated to the most commonly asked questions I receive. Since the subject of Tantra is so immense and I could never cover all the material in this book, I wanted to squeeze a little more in this way.

Q. What are chakras and do I need to know about them to practice Tantra?

A. Here is a very simple answer. There is much more to learn if you wish and might I suggest David Pond's book called Chakras for Beginners.

Chakras are energy bodies within our physical body. Traditionally there are seven of them. Starting with the first chakra, near the anus, it deals with family tribe and finances (he's such a tight ass), the second is above the pubic bone and deals with sexuality and creativity, the third is the solar plexus and deals with power (have a feeling in my gut), fourth the heart and deals with love, fifth the throat and deals with truth (frog in my throat), sixth between the eyebrows and deals with insight and seventh at the crown of your head and deals with connection to the divine.

You don't have to believe in them to practice Modern Tantra™ but you should be very aware of your body and its sensations. The value in learning about the chakras is about assisting you in having a place to focus on and experiencing feelings as you learn about energy in your body.

Q. What is a Tantra Master?

A. I believe a Tantra Master is someone who has been educated in and handed down a lineage of Classical Tantra.

Before embarking on a journey with any teacher you must educate yourself about them and their practices make sure you know what you are getting into. Please remember you do not have to get naked with your teacher and you do not have to have sex with them.

Q. What is Sanskrit and do I need to learn it?

A. Sanskrit is an ancient language used in Tantra. The words are important because they evoke a vibration when used. For higher art forms of Tantra you would want to learn some Sanskrit but for the Modern practice I am teaching it only becomes needed at a later time and then not all that many words are intoned.

Q. What has Tantra got to do with yoga?

A. Tantra Yoga is the grandfather of yogas. The yoga is the practice of opening the body to the energy forces within, a practice of preparing the body for lessons. Tantra Yoga is the wondrous vehicle which takes people safely to the other side of fearlessness, immortality, freedom, and perfection, when practiced with understanding under personal guidance of well-established Tantric Guru.

Q. I heard that chanting was something I would need to do to learn Tantra, is that true?

A. Chanting is an amazing tool of connection and healing. It is not necessary to learn to chant, but if you give it a try you will find that you will come to love it and want to use it often.

Q. I read some ads somewhere about Tantra but it looked a little sleazy, should I be concerned?

A. Always make sure you know what you are getting. The word Tantra is being used by sex workers and erotic massage therapists and if that's what you are seeking, great. Most of the time people looking for Tantric healing work or education get a big surprise when they have not asked enough questions. I do not take my clothes off in my classes and neither do my students.

Q. How do I know this love is the real thing? How do I know it's true love?

A. All love is the real thing, all love is true love. It isn't the love that should set the determination for the intent of the relationship. Love is just one aspect of many. Love is a self-state and there is no such thing as romantic or platonic love; it's all the same, it's just a matter of what intent you put to it.

Q. Why did that thing I did with my tongue that drove my last girlfriend straight over the edge to orgasm leave the next one looking at me as if I've tried to hand her a dead badger?

A. All women are different and the same woman can be different at different times. Every lover is a new experience and should be treated as such. I also encourage you to experience your long term lover as new as well and ask the questions that you should ask. Have talks outside the bedroom to determine your partner's needs and desires.

Q. How long should we wait before having intercourse?

A. I like to tell people to wait 2-3 months. It takes about this amount of time to get to know someone. If you want a relationship I say wait and don't even get too involved in making out.

Q. What's all the fuss about multiple orgasms? I fall asleep after the first one.

A. If having one orgasm is doing it for you, then don't have more than one. For some people having no orgasm works. Everyone is different and has different needs. I don't want to set goals for anyone but I do want to let people know the things that they can experience and aspire to.

Q. Why do all those spiritual people run around pretending everything is happy happy joy joy? Can't they see the problems in the world? What does spirituality have to do with the rest of us who are dealing with traffic and bratty kids and bad relationships?

A. I do not believe in wandering around in happy happy joy joy, I believe in being authentic. There are horrid things happening in the world and they make me angry. There are also sad things and happy things going on. I do know that I believe that chaos is an important part of the process of life and I think that there could never be world peace. Nothing in the universe is static and living in unbroken peace would be against the laws of the universe. We are in motion, ever changing motion which by definition means we are never going to achieve where we are going. The path to enlightenment is in the experience of existing in chaos, fully and completely aware.

Chapter Eighteen

Relationships aren't working...
Evolving a new model

Relationships: a natural connection between two or more things.

Evolving: To develop or work out: achieve gradually

With all the millions of choices we have about everything why it is that our relationship's definitions and models are so scant? We have monogamy and polyamory. Polyamory being an open relationship format where depending on agreements there can be other love or sexual partners in the mix. I understand that we have many more options when we are single but I want to address married people, or people in long term situations.

Our traditional relationship models aren't working very well anymore. I wonder if they ever really did. We have a 61 percent divorce rate and 40 million sexless couples in the US, and I suspect that it is even more dismal. About 78 percent of men and 40 percent of women will have a physical affair at some point in their marriage and the marriages with kids are in the lead. Emotional affairs can be even more damaging as they tend to last longer and have bigger consequences.

The internet has made cheating a lot easier as we can find a potential partner on line. We can create hook ups from the comfort of our own family rooms even. Women can have powerful romantic love affairs on line with men who are listening to them and appearing to be open and vulnerable.

Marriages are not working out. No matter what anyone says we should be doing, we are not doing it. It is time for a fresh perspective about relationships. Traditional relationships frequently don't talk about the hard issues and that leaves them open to fracture.

After many cheating (them not me) monogamous relationships I decided to check into the polyamory world. I talked with many poly people and found they had some of the same issues, though their ability to communicate was far superior. It has to be when you are in a model of relationship where you make your own rules of engagement. There has to be a level of trust that the agreements (vows) will be followed and that you have the ability to hear each other's truths even when it creates feelings that are difficult.

I entered into a relationship that was poly, and though it never became anything more than theoretical, we had a year of talking about what if's. I had an opportunity to come across an old interest of mine and we started talking. The flame was still there and he mentioned that he was single. I mentioned that I was alas not. Then it dawned on me, I was in an open relationship. Woo Hoo I thought. I could be with this man that I wanted. As that realization came upon me it dawned on me that it was my choice and yet all I wanted to do was go home and be in the arms of my primary partner who had granted me this freedom to choose what I really wanted to do. I told my interest thank you but no, and the spell was broken. I had the opportunity to flirt to my heart's content with my lovers blessing, and found I felt sexy when flirting and I brought that energy back home.

That particular relationship ended and left me in an interesting space. I did not really feel that I wanted to be in an exclusive relationship though I did want to have a lover. I did not want just a casual thing as with the worry about physical safety I needed to feel safe. Just so happens there was a man in my life who wanted the same thing and we embarked on a non theoretical open relationship. He had another lover. I got to go through all the conversations about being in a partnership that required scheduling, sexual safety, communication when he was with her, meeting her, not liking her, feeling like our time was limited, talking about him not bringing enough energy to the mix and a lot more. Jealousy never came up for me which I found interesting.

I found I was asking myself more questions about what I really wanted. I came to the conclusion that I didn't want monogamy, nor a poly relationship (defining poly here as being open to the opportunities that can come your way) but perhaps something more in the middle. I wanted to have a relationship that was evolving.

An evolving relationship? I ponder the concept I had created. As a person who desires growth and evolution as a way of life it seems fitting that I have a relationship model that suits that. To me evolving means just that, a relationship that is not in a box, but one with intent, clarity and communication. A relationship that dares to evolve through the years as the people in it evolve as well.

To create this model requires commitment to authenticity from the participants, and the ability to create agreements and manage them. We must be able to talk about all the hard stuff that might come up and put the relationship in the forefront. We must conduct ourselves with the utmost integrity, and the willingness to trust our own journey and process, and that we are creating a relationship from a place of fullness instead of lack and fear.

It's time to look at your relationship model and ask yourself and your partner whether it's working for you or not. Have a planned relationship talk every 6 months or so and ask the question, "Are you happy with this relationship? What is working for you and what isn't?"

This ability to be open and honest will create the bond of intimacy that so many marriages and committed partnerships are lacking today.

How to:

Ok time to get brutally honest. I will make this relatively safe by asking you to do this on your own to start. The question is, are you happy in your relationship? Not ok, or good enough, but really truly happy. Write down both what is great about the relationship and then write down what you would want to change. Be completely open and out of the box. Don't hold anything back; this is the time to be candid. If you are single then write down exactly the perfect relationship you would want.

I am not having you share this with your partner at this time because it requires some skills to exchange this information in a way that will enlighten instead of hurt. If you are having a great relationship then by all means share.

Chapter Nineteen

Sex... The Five levels to Sexual Mastery

Sex: the sexual urge or instinct as it manifests in behavior.

Mastery: possession of consummate skill

Sex is one of the most basic fundamental instincts that we have as humans, and just as important as air, food, water and shelter is the drive we have to procreate. We are driven by our hormones to mate and have babies. I know we would like to think we are more sophisticated than that, but we are ruled to a large extent by our biology. What we need to do is to educate ourselves about the ways we can utilize our biology for our better good and pleasure.

When we hit puberty we need to have a solid understanding of what is about to transpire in our bodies. Sadly we don't get truthful information about feeling like we are going to die if we don't have sex with someone. We get told that we should keep our pants on and just say no.

Listen up everyone; we are talking about the most driving force in the universe, the energy in which life is created! The energy in which poetry and music is born, and men die in battle, for sexual energy is a force of nature.

We tell our girl children that sex is something people do when they are in love. Now although that is a beautiful sentiment it's not always true. Sex and love are two very different things. Sex can happen when people are in love but it happens all the time when people aren't. When we set our kids up like that we set up the expectation that when they are turned on they must fall in love, or be in love.

Now before you go and get all upset with me let me make myself very clear. I do not advocate teen sex; I think teens should wait till they have some emotional maturity. I do however believe that the thing that is going to make a difference here is real education about the feelings we have and the power in sexual expression. We need to be taught to own our sexual energy and how to harness it and utilize it for something other than just sexual activity. Education, empowerment, honor of one's self and others, as well as the ability to talk with adults and get real information is what it takes to get teen sex and teen pregnancy under control.

Now for us adults let's think back to how or where you learned about sex. That's pretty dismal for most people. Right now there are 40 million couples experiencing sexless relationships in the US and the numbers are growing. Your sex education probably came from magazines, porn, health class, your parents, the locker room, or purely on accident. Both men and women are sadly lacking in the area of sexual knowledge, let alone sexual mastery and spiritual sexual connection.

In general what you have learned about sex is limited to the sperm and the egg and who puts what where. That is simply basic sex. Basic sex is intercourse sex and does not have to relate to getting pregnant. It is a relatively unconscious process.

Beyond basic sex today's sophisticated lover believes that orgasm is the key to great sex, she gets hers and he gets his and everyone is satisfied; and that's not true either. I call that "button pushing" sex, or "we are ok" sex. It can be what couples do to check that box in their relationship. That is what a lot of my clients come for help with, feeling like sex has become boring and dissatisfying even though everyone is "getting theirs".

There are 5 levels of sexual knowledge. You can learn Tantra and Tantric techniques to add dimension to your sex life. Most people are at Level 1, and even there they are lacking information. Obviously you can range between and back and forth through the levels, whether in the same relationship or when embarking on a new one.

I am not telling you that you have to get Level 5, although I will say that if you find yourself dissatisfied at any time with your current sexual relationship keep in mind that you have things to aspire towards.

Level 1- procreational sex

Basic sexual education: sperm meets egg and this where we put everything, basic sexual health, basic anatomy. Having sex at this level is generally unsatisfying for both partners other than the man ejaculating. It is over fairly quick and with little communication regarding enjoyment or each other's pleasure beyond the physical.

Level 2- button pushing sex

Everyone gets theirs; this level tends to focus on release of sexual tension (orgasm) for both parties. Most men and women today believe that orgasm is the ingredient to sexual satisfaction, but over time this is simply not enough. Yet for most people it's all they know. Sexual engagement at this level can be alright for awhile but eventually boredom will set in as both parties know how to get each other off with efficiency, and the routine becomes fairly well entrenched.

Level 3- exploratory sex

Here is the level where people are getting bored with the status quo. The sex toys and role playing can show up here. Affairs can happen here, or a couple decides to add other people or perhaps get into BDSM or other things that push their limits. The sex frequently still has to do with orgasm being the goal, but people here are looking for bigger and bigger charges and experiences. Being bored or numb to their basic routine, couples are looking for answers outside of themselves instead of inside.

Level 4 – awakening to conscious sex

This is where there comes an inkling that there is more out there than just sex the way it has always been. The bigger and edgier experiences are getting boring as well and at some point the high is wearing off. Always searching for something better outside is losing its appeal. This is where entering the realm of Tantra and some of its techniques becomes very interesting. With some education in this arena comes the knowledge that genital friction and getting off is only the tip of the iceberg in pleasure and lovemaking.

A person at Level 4 mastery starts to understand that connection requires intimacy and energetic intent, as well as learning to separate ejaculation and orgasm for men. Women start to see that orgasm isn't something to achieve as much as surrender to, and everyone learns to expand their capacity for pleasure.

Level 5 – Conscious Union

Here is the level of Tantric union, and the highly sought after spiritual orgasm that has little to do with your genitals. At Level 5 having your old regular orgasm seems silly, even though you can have one without touching yourself or being touched, but by simply taking a breath. At this level you practice sexual union with yourself or your partner in a way that seems holy, healing and complete. The satisfaction felt from this bonding fills you up in a way you never dreamed of. This union solidifies your relationship to the utmost. When beloveds get together to create this loving expression the energy that they feel heals them, their household and their communities. The art of sex magic is practiced here, manifesting using sexual energy and intent.

Level 5 is the level we were born to live in and love in. It does not preclude having some good old-fashioned sex when you want but it will elevate your thoughts and feelings about loving someone else and receiving and giving enormous amounts of pleasure.

How to:

Assess which level you are in right now. Most of the time we range through them, especially at the start of a new relationship. If you have a partner share your thoughts about where you two are. Have a discussion about whether there is interest in experiencing some different things in your love making. If so, move towards the education you need.

Chapter Twenty

Tantra for Business™... Building Empires

Business: The occupation in which a person is engaged

When I first started to teach Tantra for Business™ people thought I was crazy. Most people think Tantra is about orgasms and sex. They couldn't imagine what I was going to talk about in the boardroom.

Tantra is about understanding the connection between all things. I believe that is a formidable tool in the business world. Modern Tantra™ encompasses the ancient philosophies while acknowledging the technology and pace of this century.

My Inner Circle participants learn to use Tantra for Business™ and it all starts with Conscious Breath as do all the other foundations and mastery programs we teach. From the Conscious Breath practice we can begin to check into ourselves and understand what we are feeling and how we can use our emotions for creating the relationships we want in business.

People run companies and therefore people do business with other people. Most business deals are based on the intimate relationships we create with another. Intimate does not mean sexual. So when you have acquired the knowledge to harness your emotions and predicate another's you are ahead of the game.

Taking command of a board meeting requires finesse and timing, and knowing if you should indeed even do so requires uncanny observation skills. In the moments of slowing down and becoming aware of the subtle relationships occurring beneath the surface you might quickly pick up on who is who, and where you should be directing your efforts.

Being able to read the energy of another as you meet them guides you to understanding what posture and intent you should present when shaking hands or opening a conversation. Should you good old boy them, should you lower your eyes just a tad, should you dominate them immediately? These questions can be answered in one breath once you learn the skills of reading energy and body language.

There is a bubble that is usually created by the dominant party in the group, and frequently that is the leader that you want to understand. They create a bubble that everyone is either part of or on the out of. If you find yourself on the outside you would be able to step into the bubble or even take it over. If you found an important ally outside the bubble you would be able to draw them inside of it and thereby create rapport and intimacy with that person.

All this is done without talking or apparently doing anything. From an outside perspective you are simply being engaged. If we look at the definition of business we see the word engaged. Business: an occupation in which a person is engaged.

Being engaged takes all the principles of Tantra and applies them with skill and precision. These are the same skills in which we live all of life. Conduct your business with authenticity, intent and integrity while you engage people in the present moment. Manifesting your outcomes and being immensely in gratitude of those business relationships is the key to building an empire.

I have a client who owns a company called FilterSure. This company created an amazing technology that has been patented and holds the key to healing the waters of the planet, less expensively than anything else in existence. One would think that this would just take off like gang busters.

After talking with the owner I was able to pinpoint why this company was not taking off. My client had an attitude. He has worked for years to get people to listen to his spiel to no avail, and he had become frustrated. His product is desperately needed in the world today and no one was listening.

First we worked on a global vision for the company, making a statement of intent that was powerful and had emotion behind it. Then I worked with my client on rapport and speaking from authenticity and compassion.

He learned about breath work, letting go of fear and the past frustrations to become very clear about the outcome for the company. We talked about how to create the desired effect for each meeting. I am happy to say that within 4 months of working together everyone has been saying yes to my client, and the company is now securing Phase 1 contracts in niche markets that have massive revenue generating implications and getting the type of exposure from government clients and the investment community that was not happening with regularity prior to the Tantra training. This is only one of the many that we have helped to success.

Tantra for Business™ is powerful, and it will assist you in creating your empire.

How to:

"How you do this, is how you do everything" I tell my students and clients this all the time. Take a look at how you do your life; is it paralleling your business? DO you feel like a victim or empowered?

Take a moment and write a powerful vision statement for your business. Here is the one we used for FilterSure.

"Nothing is more expensive to our health, our industry and our planet than water that is dirty and dying. Without water we cannot survive, business and humanity will grind to a halt. FilterSure technology is the answer to our global dilemma, healing the water and our lives. FilterSure's applications are limitless and inexpensive. If it is in the water and we can identify it, and FilterSure technology can remove it."

Chapter Twenty-One

Union... The Tantra Dance of Sexual Loving

Union: sexual intercourse

The way most people are having sex today is basically dismal. That goes for women as well as men. I know that men can be simpler in their needs as far as sex is concerned. Give the man appreciation for his prowess, let him give his partner an orgasm or 3 and make sure he gets sex at least once a week and for the most part he won't complain... too much.

Women want more, and I am not talking about multiples here. She wants to be adored (like there is no one else on earth that could take her place), she wants to feel the intimate connection (her partner hears her and pays very close attention to her desires), she wants to feel her partner would walk through fire for her (she wants a hero), she wants a heart-felt connection in the bedroom (she is touched in a way that makes her cry from tenderness and love), and for variety she wants to be taken by a powerful being and ultimately surrender her heart and body to her beloved. Her beloved needs to be skilled in the art of pillow talk, sensitive in his hands, tongue, vajra, strong in his vitality, and knowledgeable in Tantric arts of intimacy and sexual union.

What you will read next will have an impact on you- perhaps make you hopeful or daunted. Maybe you will think it's way too unbelievable or way too corny for you to even entertain. I do want to share that what I write about is in the realm of possibility for all of us. I have taught people the path to this experience. I want you to read with an open mind and heart and to believe that everyone deserves this way of loving. This practice is not something you do every day, and it does not take away from the other things you do. All this does is add something completely compelling to your existence. Sexual union of this magnitude solidifies hope and belief that we are indeed divine within. It gives us the faith that there is God or whatever symbols of love and divinity you look to in your life.

Sexual union is the ultimate in Tantric love making. It can only be described as holding the hands of God, or experiencing the intimate connection you have to the Universe. It is deep and powerful and has the ability to profoundly transform your entire life in one experience. It is as though time has stopped and there is nothing more that is needed in the moment you are in, but the moment you are in. You have come to a complete stop of all motion except the breath. Physicality dissolves and you are left with the breath and the vibration of bliss (spiritual joy). As you let go of doing and arrive at being, the orgasm you are experiencing is beyond anything you have physically ever imagined. It has moved from the genitals to encompass your whole being and beyond. There is pure ecstatic bliss of losing oneself to time and space. This bliss can go on for hours and I have had an experience of several days.

The aftermath of such an experience is seeing the world as a newborn. Your experience of everything and how you feel and view yourself has profoundly changed. Your ability to feel in your full potential as a human has increased in magnitude, your ability to observe and understand others has heightened and your sense of compassion is magnified.

This practice of Tantric sexual union is one that takes time and patience to develop with a regular partner. You must be willing to see your dark sides as well as your light and to travel with another to a depth of vulnerability that one rarely sees today.

There are people out there today who would have you believe that you can do this with casual partners, or in a session or two with a teacher. I believe this is quite absurd. True you can use Tantric techniques to heighten your sexual pleasure and that's great. You can have extended orgasm for 4 hours and that's wonderful. What I am talking about is much more than any of that. In fact my best physical orgasm lasting for hours pales in comparison of this practice of sacred union. On a scale I liken it to a 2 (physical orgasm) compared to infinity (spiritual orgasm).

Imagine for a moment a union so profound with your beloved that the earth shifts.

Imagine feeling so complete that you need nothing else in that moment.

Imagine that you feel sanctified and holy, that you are experiencing God in the moment of Union.

Imagine you and your beloved have an experience of such magnitude that life's issues dissolve because the spiritual bond between the two of you is so intimate nothing can shatter it.

Now stop imagining and start the journey…

How to:

To start experience the intimacy of eye gazing. Sit across from each other and start to breathe with each other in harmony. If you are single then do this in the mirror with yourself. Soften your gaze with feelings of tenderness and love. Stay with one eye, don't dart back and forth. Keep the eye gaze going as you breathe with each other for at least 5 minutes. You may experience feelings and that's ok. It can be difficult to let someone in, even your lover. Do this daily.

Chapter Twenty-Two

Vajra… The Wand of Light

Vajra: the Sanskrit word for the penis, translates into the "wand of light".

Wow, is there anything on the planet that gets more attention than the male organ. We have built monuments, bullet trains, automobiles, rocket ships, missiles and architecture that resemble it.

Battles and duels have been fought, empires brought to their knees, songs and poetry written, and jokes told about it. Men are frequently seen at the mercy of their long time buddy who seemingly makes decisions without them, getting men into more trouble than the reward was usually worth.

Ah, and then there are the names men bestow upon their penis. I have heard some really funny ones in my time and I am always in wonder about this member which when potent can make a man feel exalted and when impotent can bring him to his knees in powerlessness and shame.

Most men live in awe and fear of their penis and its functions. An awe that it becomes erect and provides so much fun, entertainment and pleasure, and then an almost crippling fear when it fails to perform when needed.

As women we have bought into the awe and fear as well. There is awe of a penis attached to a man who has achieved sexual mastery and understands how to use his wand for pleasure and healing us. Then there is fear of what might happen to a man and therefore his penis should we ever need to let him know we want something different than what he is doing for us. There is also the fear of being hurt by ignorance or cruelty when a man yields his penis unconsciously or as a weapon.

I know and work with men who are suffering shame and guilt about the pain they or other men have done with their penises. This can be something like broken condoms causing abortion or as heinous as rape. No where on earth is there such a love-hate relationship than between the pleasure and pain that can be created by the mighty phallus.

In Tantra the penis is called a vajra or lingam, translating into the wand of light or the jade stalk. A man can be trained to be more conscious of his sexual energy and how to utilize it with intent and control. Instead of viewing the vajra as a separate entity with a mind if its own, it can become a true treasure indeed. Once a man has learned about self pleasuring instead of merely masturbating, and has become proficient at ejaculation mastery and full body multiple orgasms, he is stepping into the position of true sexual mastery. When the empowered and aware man makes love to his partner he understands that his wand is about love and not the start nor the end of any experience. His wand is another expression of his self, but only one part of the whole.

It is imperative that men let go of the idea that the erection and vajra are the main event of a sexual encounter. That is a very limiting belief for both parties.

There are companies making huge amounts of money by playing into men's fears about their lack of erection. The porn industry is not helping men out either. Ejaculation mastery isn't about being able to last a long time so you can pound her into oblivion and numbness. It's about the ability to receive more pleasure as a man - and that pleasure isn't about the goal of getting off. Another reason to be in control of your timing as a man is to be in the dance of love as long as both parties desire. That dance can be very still while inside, so tender that her heart heals as you create love together.

As a man I want you to take a moment and contemplate what it would be like to heal from the fear and wounds of performance anxiety. Imagine being soft and having your partner hold your vajra and jewels gently and lovingly and tell you that they love you this way. That you are loved and desired just as you are, just for being you, not having to perform in any way. Imagine that as a man you are deeply cared for and respected regardless of your erection status.

Learning through self pleasuring that your entire body is capable of extreme orgasmic pleasure takes the pressure off of performance and it changes the perspective of what sex should be like. Self pleasuring is about the whole body, moving the focus away from the vajra. Taking the time to experience other sensations in all your other parts and learning what feels good everywhere is imperative to attain sexual mastery. Through the practice of Tantra men can achieve this and much more in the area of sexuality.

In a world where a man can feel like all of his life hangs in the balance of whether or not his vajra is big and powerful enough, it has to be refreshing to understand that with some simple education and some new paradigms that's one concern he doesn't need to lose sleep over anymore.

How to:

This is how to start your journey of empowerment. Find some time for half hour to touch your whole body in a gentle and loving way. Pay attention to your whole body, not just your vajra. Bring feelings of love to yourself, honor your body that has carried you this far. After 20 minutes of doing this bring attention to your vajra and jewels. Hold them gently, do not go to your automatic pattern of touching. Do something new and loving for yourself. This is not about getting off, this is about pleasure. Repeat often and encourage your partner to help you sometimes as well.

Chapter Twenty-Three

What's with the "Woo Woo"? Do I need to go there?

"Woo Woo": freaky things that make normal people go "WHAT THE"?

A long time ago, I thought people who did yoga, thought about esoteric things and chanted were freaks. I was very traditional (or so I believed) and did not ever want to be associated with being a flake.

My upbringing was conservative even though my dad was taught voo-doo in Haiti and read palms, my mom read tarot cards. We never talked about these things much and they didn't bring them out regularly.

I was in the closet during my childhood through my early twenties, hiding my gifts and not letting anyone see me as anything other than intellectual. My gifts were the ability to feel others, to connect with animals, and to see the outcome of most situations with accuracy that was uncanny to those who knew me. I was very sensitive and had a hard time growing up in many ways. I hid behind logic and my brain.

Yet still the woo woo stuff kept finding me, as though I was drawing it to me.

People would hand me books, I would hear conversations about it, and I would always end up with someone who wanted to have a séance or a tarot reading. I denied that I had any part in the weirdo's of the world.

Because we moved so much as a family I was under cover easily, and my gifts went unnoticed for the most part. There was one big exception. There was a woman who asked me one day to take a look at her horse. I was in my late teens, having graduated from high school a few months before at 16 years old.

She wanted me to help; she said to "feel what was wrong with her horse". I was embarrassed to have been seen. I tried to evade what she was asking of me. Still she persisted and so I went to her horse and laid my hands upon it. As I took a breath and relaxed into the feeling of the horse's warm body beneath my hands I became acutely aware of the pain he felt. I let my hands move to his low back and taking another breath I allowed myself to enter the horse and smooth out the tension he was holding there. The horse took a deep breath, lowered his head, chewed and yawned. I stepped back and told the woman that the saddle didn't fit and was hurting her horse. She cried and thanked me. She tried to pay me but I wasn't up for it. Sometime later she told me her horse was back to his normal self after 4 years of decline that no one had figured out the reason for. I had been seen and it didn't kill me or them. I started the slow journey out at that point.

That journey has included many teachers, masters, self study, a five year stint of celibacy, many relationships, self actualization, many mistakes, self empowerment, tragedy, ecstasy and the mundane. It is a journey that continues even now. It continues with a powerful team behind me as we take Modern Tantra™ to the world. My team consists of my serious students. They empower my journey because of their willingness to journal and share their incredible path towards transformation. They cause me to step into greater aspects of my being and through that embrace my woo woo even more.

Beyond Sex: Tantra

It wasn't that long ago when I was teaching that I would ask the question, "who believes in energy?" and only a 1/3 of the room would raise their hands. People like me were considered pretty darn freaky. I would break out a few energy exercises and there would always be some man saying, "do I have to do any of this woo woo stuff to get laid?" Hmm well perhaps having a different way of thinking about sex would help.

I purposely did not use too many Sanskrit words or too many ideas that were really "out there". I was then and I am now catering to mainstream conservative people - for people whom I believe need this the most, which is the majority of us in the world. Now that said, I still needed to get everyone their lessons and get them on board with getting into their bodies and learning some of this Tantra stuff.

I used techniques that did stretch people's comfort zone, but I found they would rise up to the challenge.

Once the movie *The Secret* and *What the Bleep Do We Know* came out, people started to raise their hands more in class when asked about energy. Then Oprah made people like me ultra cool and today everyone believes in energy and it is not as challenging to get people to open and try new things.

I still don't use many Sanskrit words and concepts that people can object to. I believe in teaching simplicity. It is amazing really, and it works. Just like in Yoga you don't need to get all pretzeled up (go for Kundalini yoga), in Modern Tantra™ I teach classes and workshops where you don't need to learn a new language to follow.

Now I don't want you to think you can learn classical Tantra without the woo woo stuff, because you can't. But very few people will ever take the time or discipline needed to find a Master and truly study Classical Tantra anyway.

To get benefit from this book and my teachings you don't need to embrace your inner woo woo any more than you feel ready for. But

91

hey, you don't know what you don't know, and it can be kinda fun out here on the fringe… stick a toe in and give it a try.

How to:

Stand up and put your right hand in the air above your head and start shaking it for all it's worth. Then move it, still shaking to your forehead for a bit, then continue to your throat, your chest, your solar plexus, your pubic bone and then around the back to your butt. Stop the shaking and close your eyes and just feel your hands and body. Perhaps your hand has a floating feeling; if so just let it float. Open your eyes and assess how you feel, how does your hand feel different than the other? Now do the other hand. Do you feel more alive? Is your body vibrating and tingling? Great, that's energy in your power. You can learn to have your whole body feeling that way.

Chapter Twenty-Four

X-rated… Why Porn is Destroying your Sex Life

Pornography: Pictures, writing, or other material that is sexually explicit and intended to arouse sexual passion

Using internet porn is the number one sex addiction in the world and, though many think the act of using porn is not an issue I believe they are dead wrong about that. I see the use of porn destroying many relationships and cause a lack of intimacy in many others. Now I do want to clarify that looking at porn every once in awhile or watching it with your lover occasionally is different than using it so that it causes a problem in your life. If your internet porn use is a regular thing every week, or every month then there is a problem. If anyone has ever said they thought your use was a problem then it probably is.

Porn addiction is generally described as obsessive sexually related behavior that dominates the addict's life. The compulsive behavior can range from obsessive use of pornography or promiscuity, to use of prostitutes or even sexual violence.

I have no moral stance against porn. I just understand the ramifications and the fallout because I get so many emails and phone calls begging for help in getting off porn. I talk about men in this chapter though I know there are women addicted to porn as well.

Visual stimulation has been around as long as mankind has been, and even though pornography and erotica have been around for centuries it has not been the problem it is now. Scientific studies have concluded that merely seeing photos or videos of nude women will increase levels of naturally healthy glandular activity in men. However, the ability to view porn so readily over the internet has caused porn to escalate out of bounds from a pursuit of a healthy instinct to become a huge addiction problem.

Boys are computer savvy from a very early age and finding the porn is easy. One of the issues that happens at a young age when porn is used is that it is anchored or linked to intense stimulus (orgasm). The user anchors a visual to an intense stimulus over and over again, and this creates pathways in the brain that limit its ability to be as aroused by other things. Also the chemicals released create an intense high. After awhile the high from the stimulus is bigger than the high from a real experience, and people find themselves dissatisfied with real encounters and real bodies. Eventually the user can't even get aroused without porn or fantasy. Artificially induced arousal is detrimental to one's ability to truly feel anything, both physically and mentally.

Another problem is what the commercial porn industry has done to sex. It has become very fake and has no real people feeling anything real sexually. If you view it and believe that's what sex is about, it will lead to real issues in the bedroom. None of the women in porn have engorgement of their vaginas and/or any other sign of excitement. Most real women do not want to be treated as porn stars nor do they want you to act like one either.

Porn can be easier to engage in than having a real relationship that requires intimacy; porn can leave you with the inability to relate to a real person.

There are other ways we can find porn addicting as well. The litmus test for porn addiction usually revolves around shame. If what you are doing is shameful to you and that shameful feeling is what is arousing you, this is grounds for seeking help.

The term "sex addict" has been used as a punch line on television so often that it's hard to believe that it can actually be a serious addiction. For those affected however the ramifications of porn addiction are all too real, often leaving marriages, careers and bank accounts in ruins.

The effects of porn can be overcome by education, and some reprogramming. Although porn is a consuming addiction, and the "industry" has established a deep hold in modern culture, there is relief to be had from the shame or fears which tend to drive the people toward this obsessive habit.

Tantra has been mis-labeled exclusively as a sexual art. It includes sexual awareness, but only 3% of Tantra is specifically about sex.

I would urge you to stop using porn and if you can't give it up entirely at least cut out the regularity. Then start to reconnect with your own body and senses. The result of masturbating to porn is to essentially disconnect from your own experience and body.

Reconnecting to yourself, your authentic feelings both emotionally, physically and exploring your sexuality without the use of visual stimulation will enhance your sexual life. It is the path you would need to take to sexual mastery.

How to:

Well obviously I'm not here to tell you how to use internet porn. What I would like you to do is to make an honest assessment of whether or not this is a problem in your life. Take the challenge of figuring out if you can go without porn for 6 months. Experience your own sensations and your own arousal created by your mind. Do not use fantasy about anyone or anything else. Just feel your own arousal from your own touch. If this seems scary remember that you may have spent years not being in your own body and your own experience. Fantasizing and being in your head is not the same as being in your body. Check back in and learn to experience even greater pleasure than you have now.

Chapter Twenty-Five

Yoni... The Sacred Space

Yoni: The Sanskrit word for vagina, translates into the sacred space.

The universe is created in the womb of woman. Woman holds the potential for bringing life and creation to fruition. We must honor and respect the power of the feminine dance and the exquisiteness of her body.

How in the world do we make sense of our feminine bodies and their parts when our parents are too embarrassed, fearful or ashamed to use language in a loving way? How do we honor ourselves and ask our partners to honor us when our very nature is subject to disregard and disrespect? Where in society are we taught to revere the power of the Yoni, the power of the sacred space?

There are so many words used for the most beautiful flower in existence, and very few of them feel good when we use them. I won't disturb you here by citing a list, suffice to say that implications and emotions created by them range from cutesy to crude.

They are certainly not easily used in the language of love, and that relates to many problems in communication that women have in love making.

The first time our parent tells us we have a "down there" or a "woo cha ho" or our "private parts" we accept their emotional charge about it. We accept their feelings about our yoni. Maybe they feel good about themselves and they empower you to use the "proper" word vagina. Said with clinical detachment we repeat the word and the tone back and in our minds. We accept the detachment. Our vagina is to be covered, our vagina is private, we have to keep it clean or it will smell, and we have to keep it safe from others.

There is much fear surrounding the vagina. With sexual abuse rampant we want to be diligent and keep our daughters safe. From an internal perspective we understand the sanctity and the fragility of this part of the body. It houses the essence of woman, her emotions, her vulnerability and her creativity. Once she has been assaulted there may be the ability to repair her but rarely is there a total regaining of the Yoni's true subtle expression.

This fear we hold is passed along to our daughters and their feelings about their bodies. We have to provide ways to keep them safe and feeling empowered. I believe that path is about education and our own healing as parents.

You telling your daughter that she has a sacred space, a yoni, is a huge part of empowering her. Showing her through your actions and words that she is sacred and her whole body is beautiful will allow her to flourish as a whole and healthy woman. Your words should reflect the honor that you hold for your body and hers. Your actions should put forth that there is no shame, no embarrassment, no sexual charge or negativity felt towards her body or yours.

Clearly we have a lot of work to do for the coming generations.

As adult women we can embrace having a yoni, a sacred space, and start the journey to full healing. We can embark on this journey ourselves or with a partner. It is never too late to claim what is your birthright of feeling sexually empowered, beautiful, creative, aroused and mysterious.

We can change the language we have about our yoni and help our lovers do the same. When we call our clitoris our pearl we access an ease of communication. After all asking your lover to polish your pearl is amazingly sexy. We can ask for what we need and desire for ourselves and our bodies and we can use the language of empowerment to do so.

We need to first and foremost become our own best lovers. We need to become lovers to our yonis and see how amazing she is when in full arousal. Many women have never experienced full engorgement of their yonis and have no idea it is even possible. Please ladies, get a mirror and take a very long time to excite yourself and watch the beautiful flower that is yours expand and engorge as excitement fills her.

If we women took the time with ourselves or asked our men to take the time to truly and deeply turn us on we would be astounded at how much grander our yonis would feel.

Below is a personal story from a student of mine. I wish to express my thanks and gratitude to her for allowing me to print this intimate journey. She wishes that her story inspire other women and men to experience the beauty found through education which leads to healing.

How to:

"I became turned on as I was reading the most mundane document possible, some sort of brochure or something...As I stood there; I became more and more aroused, until I had to move. I was feeling very sexy with no underwear on, and in a passionate instant, I threw myself on my bed and started touching my body, semi naked. With Conscious Breath I was able to control my arousal; most of all I was in pure pleasure as I was riding those waves of arousal. I also felt the freedom to vocally express my pleasure, having no one around helped...

Moments after my yoni shed tears of sadness, gratitude, loss, rebirth, I recorded my experience, healed from the irreverence I have received and inflicted upon myself.

In deeply connecting with my sacred space I have also connected with myself in many levels and transformed my relationship to my body-my temple. I am no longer an object of pleasure, but a living, breathing, loving organism with powerful capacities to heal, be healed; give and receive pleasure.

As I lay there, right hand on yoni and left on heart chakra, my legs spread out to the world, I let my feelings work through my body. At the crest of the wounded orgasm, I felt all the sadness in my yoni rise up into my heart and I held myself there, sobbing, wailing, letting go, and healing. I sent the energy from my heart, the healing center, back to my yoni. I sent my yoni some Love. I never knew that was possible!

I cried out remnants of hurt, of misunderstanding. I let go of what I thought orgasm should be like. My teeth were buzzing, an internal tangible signal that I am aware of the connections, that I AM connected to the universe in that moment.

I looked out the windows and saw the branches of the plum tree pressed against the window, as if reaching out to me. I felt the loving vibrations, the comfort-- Mother Earth nurturing me through her children. I felt tremendous gratitude to be alive, and to feel.

Yoni is the space that reflects myself. I felt so incredibly connected to myself as I was holding my yoni, and I had no idea that I owned a sacred space where such an experience was possible. Not only was I connected to my body, my soul, my spirit, but I was also connected to the universe, the earth. I was connected to everything... I was everything… I am everything...”

Change happens in an instant.

“On this momentous milestone event, I begin my journey of conscious divine sexual exploration, in the spirit of respectful celebration. I let myself feel through the range of emotions, feelings, and let it be as it is. I do not try to suppress it or deny myself the experience. Instead, I surrender to my own experience, creating space for pleasure and blissful healing transformation, all following the breath. The body knows how to heal itself...if only we are open to it."

Chapter Twenty-Six

Zen is for Sissies... Sitting Still May not be Working

Zen: A school of Mahayana Buddhism that asserts that enlightenment can be attained through meditation, self-contemplation, and intuition rather than through faith and devotion and that is practiced mainly in China, Japan, Korea, and Vietnam. Also called Zen Buddhism.

Now here is a chapter title that is bound to raise eyebrows and more. It was meant to get your attention and even your dander up if needed. The one thing Tantrics are known for is not living in fear of others' judgment and perspectives, or even their own. Living a courageous life of personal empowerment, we don't sit around wearing a mask of serenity and loving everyone vapidly.

We are warriors of self actualization; we are courageous in the face of our darkness as well as our light. We are not afraid to be irreverent, chaotic, messy, obtuse, uncensored and downright real. Of course I am not talking about actively and unconsciously setting out to hurt others. In fact Tantrics aspire to have every exhale be completely conscious and with intent. We just aren't scared to have authentic feelings and an expression of those.

I do not acknowledge teaching that creates victims of others or ties them to one teacher or path, or those teachings that condone fear. There are many students and teachers I would call new age victims. People who have read healer 101 manuals or taken a couple of classes and then live their lives afraid of "bad" energy or the nebulous feelings they have about things or places. Frequently these people cannot live normal lives for being caught in their perceptions that they have to constantly protect themselves. When one lives in their own authenticity and empowerment there is nothing to be protected from. You are love, you are gratitude, and you are the divine and the embodiment of creation.

I am not happy about teachers who teach their students to be afraid. I believe that empowering people to be courageous and self actualizing is where it's at. People need to be inspired to become leaders and healers. Inspired to heal themselves and in that way to assist in healing the people of the world. We need to learn to feel authentically, from the depths of our souls. We need to embrace our divinity, and herein embrace the divinity in everything around us. We should dare to live our dreams out loud and seek our bliss with fierce purpose. We need, deserve and crave to live life in its entirety.

So about the Zen.

I very much respect people who are dedicated to a discipline that requires that much attention and focus. However life today is not about sitting in one place in silence, we are moving at Mach one with our cell phones in our ears. And though the practice of stilling one's mind is brilliant and needed, the ability to do that while in motion, dancing, driving, laughing, and cooking or while making love is even more extraordinary. That is the practice of Tantra. It is also the path to the

Modern Tantra™ practice that I have created and am teaching my students.

My Inner Circle students learn about Tantra of Business, of Life Mastery and Tantra of Self and Relations. They learn to live as fully empowered humans in all areas of life. Being leaders in their lives they are a source of inspiration to those people around them and become healers to others as well. When even one person lives an impeccable life in front of others, those others are bound to want to follow suit. I dedicate my life to being an inspiration in my words and actions to those around me and to create a revolution to heal the planet.

I would never aspire to sitting in one space for my life, nor will I ever settle for one emotion. I desire a full rich and textured experience, and I am living that in all ways. I believe there is too much transcendence going on, and too many people attempting to live outside their bodies. We are human, and some of you believe you chose this package and existence. We were created to feel and experience every little nuance that there is to embrace inside and outside of oneself. We were created to fully engage in the world around us with everything in it.

And that being the case, why would anyone ever aspire to live in merely a sliver of self?

How to:

Write down why you are scared to go out and get what you want and deserve. If you weren't scared what would you do right now? What changes would you make to your life? Where would you live? Dream big and then ask yourself, why you would ever want to live less than you can dream?

Additional questions for your journey

Q. I had sex with my boyfriend to create intimacy. Now I feel further away from him than ever. What went wrong?

A. Sex and intimacy are two very different things. Men often need to have sex to feel close and women need to have intimacy to desire sex. It is important to know that women and men are different in how they process and desire information. Let your boyfriend know that you love to have sex with him and that you would also love to be closer in different ways.

Q. Why do you keep telling me to work on my breath? I want to learn how to make my partner melt into a puddle of jelly, not expand my lungs.

A. Conscious Breath practice is the foundation of all things. Many spiritual practices require knowledge and a set practice of breathing. Energy follows breath and when you master your personal breath with consciousness then you can begin to learn to utilize the energy in your body. Being in command of your personal energy means you can then influence other's energy. We are all connected energetically.

Q. What's your favorite position?

A. This question made me laugh. I am assuming that they meant sexually. I mean there are many things I do that require positions. I will say that my favorite of the sexual positions are the ones that feel best in the moment. I like them all depending on different things. These include how my partner and I fit together, whether there is stillness or vigorous motion, if we want to eye gaze or not, if we are practicing Tantric union or just grabbing a quickie. My advice is to try them all and have fun doing them.

Q. How does role play fit in with Tantric sexuality?

A. I don't see role play as Tantra, though you can role play Tantrically. Anything you do with full consciousness can be a Tantric experience if you are engaged fully.

Q. My girlfriend and I like to watch porn together. What's wrong with that?

A. Nothing really providing that you do not have to do it regularly to have a good time together. Keep the use in check and make sure that you aren't using it as a substitute for getting intimate and closer in your relationship.

Q. Why do you use weird words to describe the genitals?

A. We use Sanskrit words for the genitals. I believe they are terms of respect and honor and place the correct significance on our treasured body parts. We need to feel more empowered about our genitals and have words which are easy to use.

Q. What's the one thing I need to know about my boyfriend's penis that will make me a better lover?

A. Asking him that question is the best place to start. After that understanding that men feel pressure to perform and please you, and that most men are scared that one day their penis won't do what it is supposed to, and you will be disappointed. It's important to tell him how much you love him and appreciate his wand, of course be sincere. Ask him to show you how he loves to be touched and then show him you understand.

Q. What's the one thing I need to know about women so that my lovers never forget me?

A. Women are complex and no two are the same. To be unforgettable as a lover can work two ways. You didn't specify whether you wanted them to have fond memories or not so that's the first place to start. To have women remember you fondly you must really love women. That does not mean you are heterosexual and want to have sex with them. It means that you love the feminine and love all aspects of women. It means you respect and adore women. Men who feel that way have no lack of women surrounding them. To be an unforgettable lover requires understanding that your penis is not the main event in love making, understanding that women want to have a heart connection, they want artful pillow talk, they want to feel safe and they want to be adored. Learn Tantric Sexual Mastery and you will be confident that you will always be remembered fondly.

Q. My penis is too small. Is there anything I can do about that?

A. Let me say that out of all the women who have complained to me about their partner's size over the years, only a very small percent said he was too small. That said if you indeed feel too small the answer is yes, you can do something about that. You can do surgery and a whole host of really ugly things to yourself or you can try these two things. One you can learn about energy and use it to make yourself very big when inside her. Two you can learn the ancient art of enlarging your actual physical size. This is not a myth and it is very effective though the process takes dedication. I have an ebook on this subject of sexual vitality and enlargement.

Q. My mom says Tantra is against Christianity. Is it?

A. No, Tantra is not against anything. It is a philosophy and a study of the universe and of how to love each other better. I teach plenty of Christian people this art form, and it is especially necessary if you desire a long term monogamous relationship that is sustainable and passionate.

Q. Can polyamorous folks practice Tantra, or is it just for monogamous couples?

A. Anyone can practice the techniques of Tantra. It is a solo journey to start and then you can begin to share with a partner as you progress. It is a personal experience however and you need not ever have a partner if you don't desire one. You can have multiple partners as well. However I do not think that Tantra can be practiced with casual encounters other than to bring some of its techniques to the mix. Tantric sexual union takes a long-term intimate relationship between the two practicing.

Q. How do I regulate intensity levels in myself pleasuring?

A. Conscious breathing is the key to all things Tantric and really to an awakened life. This question is usually asked by men when they embark upon ejaculation mastery. As well as knowing all the physical cues a man must be aware of his energetic state. When self pleasuring a man will bring himself up to a level 9 (out of 10) or higher in intensity, maintaining the ability to remain in that pleasure without ejaculating. To regulate the intensity the man must use his breath at the right times.

Q. What do you say/do when your child walks in on you having sex?

A. Most of the time you don't need to say or do anything. All you really need to do is to not freak out, just remain calm and acknowledge the child and then see what they want. Kids will ask the questions they need to ask when they need to ask them. If they walk in and ask about what you are doing simply say you are making love. Depending on how old they are they will ask more about that or not. This is an area that we are going to address in our teachings. Parents need to know how to communicate these topics easily and without shame or embarrassment so their children can grow up sexually healthy.

Q. How do I find the MAN that I want?

A. This one is easy. Be the woman that will attract the man he is. As to finding him, he probably won't be delivering the pizza so get out and live the life you want full-on, with passion and integrity. He will be right around the next corner.

Q. How do I show a man how to love me? Well if he's a MAN, shouldn't he already know?

A. The art of a great relationship is to always provide opportunities for success. Let your man know when he pleases you. Be open to communicating your desires and the things you need to feel loved, adored, sexy and heard. He should do the same. We have a protocol when teaching couples about success and it works great! No man knows everything you need automatically and if he does, don't assume he always will. We can all use a little help to be successful.

Q. How do I introduce concepts of Tantra to my partner who is very rigid in his beliefs system?

A. Introducing anything new to someone who isn't interested doesn't work. The best way to live life is on your own accord. If you start the practice of Tantra, there will be change in your relationship. It is always risky to change the status quo, but if you were happy to remain where you were then you wouldn't be asking this question. Go slow and make your changes and then be open to answer questions and concerns.

Q. How do we practice safe sex using Tantra? Isn't the full experience of intimacy generally going to cross safe boundaries, related to sharing fluids, either oral stimulation or even immersion, men's and women's ejaculation, etc.

A. The reality is that safer sex is an imperative for the physical safety of self and others. And yes, full expression of intimacy would be hindered by all the needed safety measures. This is why for the deep Tantric practices you should be a fluid bonded couple.

Q. How does one state that they are an Atheist and still come to a sense of Divine Awareness through Tantra?

A. Interesting question… I suppose that would be dependent on the individual's definition of the word Atheist. If it were simply a matter of not believing in God then one can still come to the understanding of being one with everything, being connected in the grander expression of life. Perhaps even to come to the conclusion that there is nothing but self, as long as the awareness comes.

Q. So you can lie down next to somebody and move energy and have an orgasm?

A. Yes. You would have to have a good foundation and practice to start. It shouldn't take too long if you have the right teacher.

Q. So you can lie down next to somebody and move energy and make them orgasm?

A. Yes and it is helpful if they have a solid foundation as well.

Q. So you can make somebody orgasm without touching them?

A. Yes, I can.

Q. I thought guys needed physical touch to orgasm; I thought only girls could without.

A. All of us are capable of energetic orgasms, those are orgasms that can occur without being touched physically and one that may or may not experience the physical symptoms of arousal. We are even all capable of physical orgasm that requires no physical touch. Ain't life grand!

Q. So isn't Tantra just sex positions?

A. No it isn't. Many people confuse the Kama Sutra and Tantra, though the Kama Sutra isn't only about sexual positions either.

Q. What's the purpose in the attempt to exchange energy?

A. Intimacy and connection, super charging sexual energy or heart energy. Really any exchange of energy should have intent in the forefront. So the purpose is what you intend. When I teach Tantra for Business the energy exchange will be for a different purpose than with a lover.

Q. Why is it not awkward when you're staring at someone?

A. It would be awkward if you were staring at someone. We eye gaze which is softer and usually carries a heart connection. Soul gazing is even deeper and happens when both parties engage with consciousness. Allowing someone to truly see you is a very intimate practice and much of Tantric sexual experiences use this.

Q. Is there a point when it gets to be too much when you want to lunge at each other and do it?

A. Yes, and yet the beauty in Tantra is learning to build even more arousal and expand your capacity beyond what you know is even possible.

Q. Is it possible to conduct energy work using the Lingam as a Wand of Light if there is a Condom on? Doesn't the rubber prevent or adversely affect the energetic flow?

A. I have heard some people believe this but I have not found this to be the case.

Q. What's the story with anal sex? How does this relate to the desires men have and is this a perverse act, or a naturally pleasurable activity that is misunderstood, or...?

A. All the body has the capacity to be pleasured. The anus is no different than the elbow or the mouth. In fact in men it is pretty imperative they get on friendly terms with their prostate gland. There is a huge problem going on today with men and their prostates and that's translating into issues with sexual function. Regular prostate massage either by self or a partner is going to assure more prostate health.

Q. I have heard (according to Stephen Chang, author of The Tao of Sex) that there is nothing quite so formidable as finding a lover whose genitals fit together naturally, without being too wide, too long, too deep, or whatnot. I realize the Yoni is amazingly resilient as well as strong enough to envelop a man whose genitals are small, but how does one work with a set of mismatches in the genital area, such as giant vajra/tight yoni, or extremely loose/wide yoni and small-side-of-average man. Does it mean that people should break up if their physical selves aren't naturally jiving? Wouldn't a large man eventually want to connect fully and deeply in the physical sense with his partner, "all in"?

A. An excellent query. It is true that fitting together well is a wondrous thing and that when it doesn't happen it can lead to issues in the bedroom. Most of the complaints I get are about the man being too big. As to the yoni, it can be tightened as need be so there is rarely a man who is too small. I know that society right now lacks the education to understand that we would work better if we physically fit our partners. I doubt anyone is going to go to that extent to break up but if we could figure out how to write better online profiles to reflect this aspect we might be on to something.

Q. Is it true that Men's highest levels of orgasm are really achieving Multi-Orgasmic states with distinct peaks and valleys? This is normally attributed to women...

A. Multi -orgasm is a terrific achievement for most men but it is not the pinnacle of pleasure or the highest level a man can attain. Once a man has mastered the art of ejaculation mastery and can orgasm without ejaculation he learns to become multi-orgasmic. After that achievement is the energetic and spiritual orgasmic states. I would like to state that these experiences not only benefit the man but are essential for the women in their lives. For women to achieve their highest pleasure men have to become masters of Tantric sexuality.

Q. What is Tantra's position on the chemistry of Amrita? In my experience it is glandular (contains hormones), mucoid-like vaginal secretions, and also may have urea. Is it "essence" like the Native Americans Indians say it is "Moon Flower Water" or is it special ejaculate, such as a feminine version of men's sperm, or what is going on? The medical community absolutely discredits Amrita as anything other than specially derived and delivered urine.

A. Women can and do ejaculate however let's approach this with some common sense. The glands that the fluid comes from are very tiny. How in the world would they be producing copious amounts of fluid flying through the air and soaking everything in sight? I believe that amrita (women's ejaculate) is created from glands and that it is indeed a special substance that is not urine. I also believe that the ejaculation we see on most porn or videos is a party trick and comes from the bladder. Betty Dobson, known as the mother of masturbation, talks about myths and truths on female ejaculation on her website. She personally knows most of the women who are the stars of these videos and knows how they prepare for their appearances. Either way I tell my students and clients that if they are enjoying themselves it doesn't matter what they are doing, keep having fun. And as with everything else don't put pressure on a woman to achieve one more thing.

Q. How does a man who wants to be a great lover embrace his feminine sexual side? Many men will state that they are in touch with their feminine side and they even bought their lover a strap on to use on them... but what we're really questioning is how does a man develop his feminine sexual side... Using Candles rose petals, and other elements of rituals that women typically understand as just naturally part of lovemaking, whereas men have to read about it... what can be done about this gap in understanding without seeking to change the nature of the man?

A. Both men and women need to be able to dance the dance of masculine and feminine with equal ease. Getting to that place does not require a strap-on. It does require the ability to seek the pleasures in both aspects. As women we go out into a man's world in the corporate arena and we are called to action applying our masculine powers of doing. I know it can be a struggle to come back to our partners and step into a space of being. I believe that we are suffering from a polarity issue in relationships. Without being in opposition we cannot create passionate attraction. There are watered down men and amped out women. The true nature of man is a warrior and the true nature of women is the goddess and until we can embrace this we are going to suffer in the bedroom.

To get to the space of embracing his feminine side a man must explore the art of surrendering. This is not submission. A man must be able to receive adoration and love even when he is not erect, most importantly when he is feeling vulnerable. He can receive by lying against the breast of his woman who is in a space of compassion for him. He can just simply explore the art of being versus doing.

What's next? Our special offers for you

After reading this book you may be asking yourself where you go from here. Here are all these amazing concepts and ideas you want to put into practice.

I have a gift for you.

The purchase of this book entitles you to 10 percent off on any of our personal coaching programs, or a workshop and a free month on our membership site.

Go to http://www.learningtantra.com/amazing-life/ and get your special coupon code today! Then go to www.learningtantra.com and look for coaching or workshops, sign up and use your code at the check out.

We also have a FREE gift for you on that page, enjoy!

We look forward to assisting you with your journey to an astounding experience as you embrace your full human potential.

Who is Team Tantra from Modern Tantra™?

Just as it takes a village to raise a child, it takes a tribe (team) to fuel world transformation. I believe in the concept of tribe and the power of creating with others. I have manifested a group of incredibly talented people to make up Team Tantra. They are on the Inner Circle of Modern Tantra™ and their efforts inspire and drive this business. I am grateful for their time and their belief in me and our mission and all the amazing gifts they bring to the table.

And though the team changes and evolves with each passing year there is one constant.

I am blessed to be on this journey with my true love Max. He is an amazing tech wizard and without him I could not accomplish as much and as quickly. He is the designer and technically brilliance behind the brand new websites we have coming and everything tech we are doing. I am eternally grateful.

"If there is one person in the world I can trust to call it like it is, and master an effective solution at the same time- it's Tanja. Using insight and understanding to model compassion in a new way, she establishes a new accountability to the essential elements in relationships, business and personal. Success follows the simple formulas that we often overlook due to our patterns and beliefs about the way things should be, instead of the way things are. I always look for the WOW experiences; seeing her do this with me and lead others to succeed in this way is completely miraculous! 'Thank you for being an exquisite woman, a marvelous teacher, a very wise and very incredible master whose sense of the world is profound'."

Max Bellasys, Executive Director and Educator

Testimonials From clients and students

"Tanja has helped me face some big issues - I realized limiting beliefs that no amount of self -improvement and seminars (including Tony Robbins) could do." Cheyenne K (23), Vancouver B.C.

"I have been a member of Tanja's Inner Circle since early this year (2009)and it has been an amazing journey. There have been bumps along the way, some big ones, but it has paid dividends. With Tanja's knowledge, patience, and persistence, real progress has been made. I have basically turned from a glass-half-empty person to a glass-half-full person as a result of working with Tanja. It hasn't always been easy, but it has been worth it." Bob Moore, Wa

"Tanja, I am writing this to tell you that I am beyond excited, amazed, and full of joy. I cannot find the words to completely describe the sense of pure freedom I am now experiencing. All fear is gone! I've been going to your workshops, following your teachings and doing what you recommend and some of the time not understanding any of it...but I did it all anyway because I sensed I could trust you.

I can't explain exactly how or when it happened but, my senses are now alive, I feel I am totally living in the fullness of the human experience and...I now TRUST MYSELF!

I just walk around all day with this little smile on my face. I began with the idea that I wanted to learn about sex. I had no idea I would get a lifetime transformation out of this AND I now understand how all of this transfers over to unbelievable sex. I get it! How can I properly thank you for something like this. You've not only touched me profoundly, but all my clients and everyone they come in contact with as well. More people must know about you and what is possible...and very doable. My deepest gratitude", Craig Sigl, Mental Toughness Trainer www.CraigSigl.com

"This past Thursday I appeared on Tanja Diamond's radio show Tantra, Love, Sex and Intimacy. I was extremely impressed with her knowledge, intuition, passion and enthusiasm for her show. Her ability to bring out the best in someone and to share that knowledge was very evident from the first minute of the show. Her mantra of "be amazing" has never been more needed than today. I look forward to many more discussions with Tanja. She is amazing". David Brooke, The Productivity Coach. www.thebrooker.com

"I am involved in Tanja's Inner Circle program (2009) and I truly can't say enough about Tanja and the program in how it has enlightened and improved my quality of life. The teachings she has given me have improved all areas of my life, being able to free myself from destructive behaviors, shame and fear. Tanja has shown me the way to change beliefs in myself to create passion and love in my life for myself and others while living in fearless integrity. Tanja is truly amazing. I highly recommend Tanja's courses to anyone who wants to empower themselves to setup and succeed in life." Dan Mellon, Vancouver, BC Canada

"Tanja is an amazing individual with a incredible gift to inspire and captivate an audience of men. The impact she made at the Ultimate Transformation 2008 Super Conference was phenomenal. I thank her for her contribution to the event as a speaker, a role model, and as a friend." Stefan Pylarinos www.lifestyletransformations.com

"As I search my memory for those on my A list, Tanja surfaces first. It was immediately apparent to me as well as the other trainees, that she embodies every attribute one needs to be in truly in service of this work...absolute personal and professional integrity, a spiritual being, honest, compassionate, and highly skilled. Tanja exhibits each of these with a great sense of humor added to ones process of discovery."-Jewel Source School Tantra Graduate, 2002 California

"With only a few scattered YouTube video clips, Tanja has given me an experiential knowledge that has added both life and power to every touch I make. ...the idea that my touch should carry "intention", in and of its self, was a quantum leap for me. I judge people by the results of their actions, not just the content of their words; the "results" of knowing Tanja has been an enriched life. Thank you Ms. Diamond!" June 7, 2008 Rodney Hamm

"Tanja Diamond will awaken your energy. She has dedicated her life to sharing the healing practices from many traditions to those ready to wake-up and live a life filled with energy and love. Get ready to get plugged in and turned on..."- David Pond, www.reflectingpond.com Astrologer/author/speaker

"Tanja, Prior to meeting you in person once and through telephone calls and emails over the past four months, I have undergone what can only be described as a transformational metamorphosis. After many years of marketing and promoting my patented water filtration technology and meeting with nothing but accumulated rejection or insanely ridiculous offers that were designed to squeeze me out of my company when I "knew" I had the 'better mousetrap" made me very angry. That anger was evident to all that I came in contact with.

Consulting with you has exponentially diminished the anger and replaced it with compassion and grace which is translating into contracts {witness the latest press release} and investment suitors. The conscious breathing and focus when meeting clients has made them exceptionally receptive to what my technology offers. It's wonderful to behold. I look forward to the rest of this grandiloquent journey."- Faith, Ron McIlwain, President Filtersure Inc.

"Tanja's Tantra class. On a recent afternoon, I was privileged to attend one of Tanja Diamond's Tantra-for-couples classes. In a small, nondescript conference room in downtown Vancouver, seven couples had gathered. The couples ranged in age and experience. The male half of one duo had been practicing Tantra for the last 10 years, while another pair had no what they were getting into. They were the winners of a radio contest. But more on them later.

I'd been to Tanja's men's class, so I kind of knew what to expect. I knew, for instance, that she'd talk about breathing, that she'd demonstrate how to kiss and touch with intent, and that we'd be told about the different kind of orgasms open to both men and women by following tantric practices. I had found those classes educational and inspiring.

They had included some intense moments, but they hadn't prepared me for the overwhelming experience of the couple's class. By the end of the session, which included a healing ceremony, husbands and wives, girlfriends and boyfriends, even some people paired up for the first time, were touching each other and holding hands in a more loving, intimate way than when we'd first come in. Many were in tears.

Perhaps the most profound effect was felt by the woman who had won the class through the radio contest. "This is so outside the box for me," she said at the end, shaking her head. It's a tribute to Tanja Diamond's positive energy and effectiveness as a teacher that this woman and her partner not only stayed for the whole four-hour class, but seemed to get as much out of it as those who came in with minds and hearts already open." Shawn Conner, freelance writer, Vancouver B.C

"Hi Tanja: Thanks yet again for your amazing help. You have the ability to read my wife and I with such speed, insight and then provide graceful feedback. I think the two hours Sunday morning were the most valuable I have spent on our relationship. I am very hopeful for the future."- Herman, Seattle, WA

"We saw Tanja because we hadn't been intimate in 8 years, I was ready to have an affair or just walk out the door. We had been through years of talk therapy already and gotten nowhere. With Tanja's help I heard my wife talk about her needs that hadn't been met, and she was able to hear me. Through the sexual healing practices I learned to awaken my wife's desires and create safety for us both. I was able to heal through her touch as well. How can we thank someone for not only saving our marriage, but teaching us to have the best sex we have ever had in our lives! Tanja, you're a marvel...." Ken and Marie, Kemore, WA.

"Tanja has certain energy under her control that one can quickly associate with calmness and love. Tanja connects deeply with people and always has encouraging motivational words. I very much enjoy being someone she considers a friend." - Lane Pierce, Master Practitioner and Trainer of Hypnosis, NLP, and Time Empowerment Techniques

"Tanja distinguishes herself as a tantric practitioner through great integrity and commitment to healing. The way she comes from her heart, wisdom and grounded knowledge and her work has been inspirational to me. I enjoy and grow by learning from and with Tanja in my own tantric journey"- Dr. Elsbeth Meuth, Director Tantra Nova Institute Chicago, IL www.TantraNova.com

"Tanja is one of the most incredible healers I have met in my journey of healing and being healed. Her rituals include aspects of healing that she has intuited from listening to what you say or don't say, how you hold your body, how you behave during ritual and much more. In other words, she knows how to get to the core issue with ease and grace, she holds the space so you feel safe to let happen what needs to happen. My experience of being healed by her, and working with her healing others, has always left me in awe of her ability, her compassion and her willingness to be there. I would not hesitate to recommend Tanja as a healer or a guide to anyone."- Lynette Littlerose, Principal Consultant and Founder Vision Amour International Melbourne, Australia

"I feel more brave and determined to move through the edgey places as a result of working with Tanja and the exemplary model she is" Anne Douglas, Banff, AB, Canada (2-18-08 workshop in Vancouver)

"I was recently on the radio show Tantra, Love, Sex and Intimacy, with Host- Tanja Diamond. I really had a "G"--reat time; Tanja had a positive and reassuring approach to all areas of sexuality. She was very gentle and humorous, having sound knowledge in all areas, yet focusing more on the Tantric side of sexuality... I gained a lot of insight just being on her show. Michael Schuessler, Author of; "The Holy G-rail" www.theholyg-rail.com

"Greetings from Tantra north. I wanted to follow-up on last weekend's event to comment a little on the 'experience'.

First let me say it was terrific to be a room with others so motivated to do something positive about their relationships - Energy in Focus! None of it could have occurred without your preparations to make it a safe place to talk, listen and learn. This was equally true for the men's session as for the couples.

Probably next for me was the frankness of your presentation - without the 'woo-woo' you referred to. You repeated in both sessions that this was very much an introduction to Tantra of which sex was only a small part. I felt definitely here was something I could investigate further should the interest arise, and in the meantime I would hear some practical advice to improve this very important aspect of my relations with my partner Barbara.

Breathe, connection, intent, be in the present raised my awareness of the attentiveness required of being together.

Lastly, I learned something special with the 'healing' rituals, goddess recognition - that among total strangers there was an ability to cast a caring and positive 'spell'. I saw in the many pairs of eyes of the women who shifted by: fear, hurt, vulnerability, desperation, caring, love, tenderness, hope and a flood of emotions.

A magical moment, for which I could not imagine I had any special talent, was holding the hands of a young woman and by your guidance recognize those hands and that person's emotional charge.

What happened was this: First the hand-holding was awkward. I changed my grip mostly to let her hands rest in mine rather than being held. Then I recall lifting them slightly just to convey the honor and respect intended by your message. At some moment while I raised my eyes from her hands I could feel her letting something go. I looked at her face and tears were streaming down her cheeks.

It was as if some huge burden had been lifted and this was one moment when whatever held her shifted and got out. My positive thought while witnessing her tears was to convey 'goodness' - to let that thought flow as freely as her tears. I was humbled to feel a part of another's deepest emotions.

So maybe some of the 'woo-woo' comes as a bonus! It was fascinating. This was overall one grand experience. I expectantly await Mastery II" Dana, Vancouver, BC

"Thank you for the couple's intimacy workshop this past weekend. I was about to give up on my relationship but now I feel like we've been reborn as a couple. Those simple exercises recreated our connection and made me feel like I can deal with all the little stuff much better now. The most amazing thing to me was how much he 'got into it'--not easy for an engineer, I think. He got a million brownie points for participating so fully!" Thanks again, Jane S. Wa

"Tanja Diamond is a healer and leader in nurturing and developing human potential and sexual transformation. When others in the world of Tantra focus on masking old Western techniques and approaches with Eastern language and empty actions, Tanja is actually an experienced and legitimate teacher working with others to embrace the craft and art of being a fully awakened human." Jeff L. www.archetypecoaching.com Washington

"It is shocking how we are so timid about expressing our aspirations. You rise above the norm as an example of exuberance. I recognized the possibility of dropping contraction (the baggage, the story, the past) and choosing expansion (love, acceptance). As for the hands-on, healing portion of yesterday, yes please. I'll give and take this as a way of life. The sexual connection in neutral is boundless. From a movement, dancer, actor person I once learned there are three possible movements a person can make: out, in and neutral. Now there is confirmation of this observation from another discipline." Expanding, Greg N, LA, CA

"I honestly can't say enough about Tanja. The tools she has given me have helped me to improve all areas of my life. I'm much more aware of my surroundings and it has helped me in ways I would have never imagined. The skills go far beyond the bedroom and have helped me become a better person. Tanja is an amazing person and I'm truly thankful to have met her. Tanja teaches in a manner that is practical and easy to implement. The realm of tantra can obviously be extremely complicated, but Tanja's students are able to immediately implement her teachings and start living a better life. I will definitely be taking more of her courses in the near future!" Jason Rude, Executive Coach, Vancouver, Wa www.lifestyletransformations.com

"Tanja Diamond makes her expertise in relationships so down to earth and fun that it's easy to open up when you are in her presence. She loves life and is full of passion to empower both men and women with their sexuality and sensuality, bringing creativity and trust to sex and intimacy. Amazing work Tanja! Keep on shining out your fabulous light with humor and joy, and thank you for your refreshing new vision." Yvonne Oswald www.globalwelcome.com Author of Every word has power.

Bibliography...Works Cited

Tigunait, Pandit Rajmani. *Tantra Unveiled*. New York: Reed Business Information Inc. 1999.

Laurel. *American Heritage Dictionary*, New York: Bantam Doubleday Dell Publishing Group. 1994

Elamn, Dave. *Hypnotherapy*. Glendale: Westwood Publishing Company. 1984

Ruiz, Don Miguel. *The Four Agreements*. San Raphael: Amber-Allen Publishing. 2001

Eker,T Harv. *Secrets of The Millionaire Mind*. New York: Harper Business. 2005

Thomashauer, Regena. *Mama Gena's School of Womanly Arts*. New York: Simon & Schuster. 2003

Pond, David. *Chakras for Beginners*. Woodbury: Llewellyn Publications. 1999

Odier, Daniel. *Desire; The Tantric Path to Awakening*. Rochester: Inner Traditions. 2001

Wikipedia, http://en.wikipedia.org/wiki/Gratitude, 3 September 2009

Emmons, R. A., & Crumpler, C. A. *Gratitude as a human strength: Appraising the evidence*. Journal of Social and Clinical Psychology. 2000.

Layden, Mary Anne, Ph.D. *"Cyber Sex Addiction"*. Advances in Cognitive Therapy: September 2005

Workshops and Coaching Programs

We have workshops and coaching for men, women and couples.

For more information and for full description, dates and sign ups get to

http://www.learningtantra.com/workshops-tantra-workshops-mens-tantra-workshops-womens-tantra-workshops-seattle-tantra-workshops-2/

Sometimes you can't get away for a workshop but need some help, and we do offer coaching programs as well as one on one phone consultations.

http://www.learningtantra.com/coaching-tantra-coaching-sessions-tantra-skype-sessions-life-coaching-business-coaching-life-coach-tanja-diamond/

I can also be hired to come to your location for private work, or you can host your own workshop.

Contact me personally for more information

Tanja@learningtantra.com

Conclusion

It is my fondest wish that you made it through the whole book and actually put the how tos to use.

Hundreds of people have already embraced empowering their lives using the techniques in this book and are living happier and more fulfilling experiences as we speak.

You can do it! You can take a step towards the life you desire! All it takes is the willingness to take a step in the direction of doing something more than you are doing right now.

If you are on the couch, get off it! Jump around and do something unexpected. You will be surprised at what happens when you make a move.

If you can't get off the couch or out of the chair then BREATHE! Anyone can do that. All of these things are motion in action. Once you make one change others will happen in your life.

If you are alone create your own tribe or family. Find other people who are alone and join forces. Help each other to make the changes you would like to see.

I truly and completely desire for you to have the life you deserve and I trust this book has been inspiring. I know that all of us at Team Tantra are cheering for you and we can't wait to hear how you are doing.

And remember, Be Amazing...

Medical and Therapeutic Disclaimer

The advice and exercises in this book can and will change your life. You should be prepared for this. There can be big emotional shifts that occur.

Common sense and good judgment should be used for both the physical and emotional aspects presented.

This book is for informational purposes only. It is not a substitute for medical care or psychotherapy. If you are in need of medical care or psychological counseling please see a licensed professional.

Follow the advice of your health care provider if you are in treatment.